Do It Afraid

STUDY GUIDE

EMBRACING COURAGE IN THE FACE OF FEAR

JOYCE MEYER

Faith Words

NEW YORK NASHVILLE

FaithWords
Hachette Book Group
1290 Avenue of the Americas, New York, NY 10104
faithwords.com
twitter.com/faithwords

First Edition: September 2020

FaithWords is a division of Hachette Book Group, Inc.
The FaithWords name and logo are trademarks of Hachette Book Group, Inc.

The publisher is not responsible for websites (or their content) that are not owned by the publisher.

The Hachette Speakers Bureau provides a wide range of authors for speaking events. To find out more, go to www.hachettespeakersbureau.com or call (866) 376-6591.

ISBN: 978-1-5460-2632-7 (trade paperback)

Printed in the United States of America

LSC-C

10 9 8 7 6 5 4 3 2

CONTENTS

HOW TO USE THIS STUDY GUIDE

This study guide is designed as a companion to the book *Do It Afraid*, and you will need a copy of that book in order to use this one most effectively. The book contains many lessons, principles, and stories that empower you to confront any fear you encounter. This study guide will help you maximize these teachings and apply them to your life as you move forward on your journey to freedom.

As you read in the introduction to *Do It Afraid*, "Fear is everywhere, and it affects everyone. It has been around since the beginning of time, and it will be here as long as the earth remains. Fear rules many people, *but it doesn't have to be that way*" (emphasis added). The main point of *Do It Afraid* is that you do not have to allow fear to dictate your decisions or determine what you will or will not do. You are free to be led by the Holy Spirit and to do everything God calls you to do. He has an amazing plan for your life, a plan our enemy, the devil, tries to keep you from fulfilling, often through fear. There may be times when you will feel fear, but if you learn to do it afraid, whatever *it* may be in your life, you will break fear's hold over you and find freedom to live a life of peace, strength, joy, and great fulfillment.

This study guide reinforces the material in *Do It Afraid*. As you read each chapter in the book, you can complete the corresponding material in this study guide. In each chapter of this guide, you will find the following sections:

Setting Your Mind on Victory: Our battle against fear has existed for thousands of years. We have much to learn from individuals from different eras in history and various walks of life who have come before us and can offer us insight and wisdom about finding victory over fear. Preceding each chapter of *Do It Afraid*, you will find a quotation related to the subject of the chapter. In this study guide, these quotations are repeated and followed by questions about how these words of wisdom can equip you to better wage your battle against fear.

Doing It Afraid: People have found freedom from fear in many different ways. Each chapter of *Do It Afraid* is preceded by a personal story from someone who has "done it afraid." After you read each one, the "Doing It Afraid" section of each chapter of the study guide gives you a chance to reflect on the story and answer questions about how it inspires you and gives you courage to press through any fear you may have.

Fear-Fighting Truths: Each chapter of *Do It Afraid* contains beneficial lessons and practical advice on overcoming fear. "Fear-Fighting Truths" offer brief summaries of the key points in each chapter, along with an opportunity for you to mark the truth(s) you feel you most need to believe and apply to your life.

Taking Courage in the Word: No book on earth gives you courage like God's Word. *Do It Afraid* is filled with powerful scriptures that will enable you to win your battle with fear. In the "Taking Courage in the Word" sections, you'll be encouraged to interact with God's Word in a variety of ways that will help you live with faith and courage.

Moving Forward in Freedom: These sections throughout the book allow you to apply what you've learned by answering questions designed to help reinforce or expand your understanding of the teaching in *Do It Afraid* and give you an opportunity to reflect on your personal journey of freedom from fear.

Keep This in Mind: At the end of each chapter, a short excerpt from *Do It Afraid* or a brief summary of the chapter's takeaway, along with a scripture, provides you with an important principle to remember and incorporate into your life as you live in victory over fear.

May God bless you as you go through this book and take important steps that will establish you in a new place of strength, boldness, and freedom.

Setting Your Mind on Victory

Courage is not an absence of fear, but an act of the will to move forward in the presence of fear.

David duChemin

Have you ever thought of courage as the absence of fear? If so, how does this statement cause you to view courage differently?

_____

_____

_____

When you think about moving forward in the presence of fear, how do you feel on a scale of 1–10, with 1 being "nervous and hesitant" and 10 being "empowered and eager"? There's no right or wrong answer!

_____

_____

_____

_____

Fear-Fighting Truths

These are the key truths from the introduction. Check the ones you most need to believe and apply to your life.

- Fear is everywhere, and no one is immune to it.
- Fear will never completely disappear from every aspect of your life, but with God's help, you can confront it and break its power over the way you think and live.
- Many people live their entire life under the tyranny of fear. They allow fear to make decisions for them, which means they never become the people they long to be and the people God created them to be.
- Fear operates in a variety of ways, including intimidation. Understanding how fear operates in your life will help you confront and conquer it.
- Fear will control you to the greatest degree that you allow it to do so. With God's help, you can choose not to submit to it; you simply need to exercise this choice.

Taking Courage in the Word

Jesus declares in **John 8:32** that the truth will make us free. How has learning the truth about something brought freedom to your life?

_____

_____

_____

John 10:10 lists three ways the enemy works to prevent progress in our lives. What are they? How has the enemy tried to use these strategies to impact something in your life—perhaps a relationship, an opportunity, or your ability to pursue a God-given dream?

_____

_____

_____

Fill in the blank: According to **1 John 4:18** (KJV), "Fear hath _____ _____." How has fear affected your life in this way?

_____

_____

We learn from **2 Timothy 1:7** that the spirit of fear does not come from God. What does God give us?

_____

_____

Moving Forward in Freedom

The introduction to _Do It Afraid_ makes several important observations about fear and the ways it keeps us from being the people God has created us to be. Which ones teach you something new about fear? Which ones are true for you or describe the way fear has operated in your life?

_____

_____

In what ways has fear kept you from becoming all God intends for you to be or held you back from doing something you believe God wants you to do?

_____

_____

How has fear influenced the way you relate to other people or caused you to feel intimidated in certain situations?

_____

_____

Is fear trying to push you around or dictate a certain decision in your life? How can you move forward in faith instead of allowing fear to hold you back?

_____

_____

Think about a situation in which you felt intimidated, and ask God why you felt that way. If the answer comes to you quickly, write it here. Remember that it may not come to you right away, but once God reveals the truth to you, it will help you take steps toward freedom from that fear (John 8:32).

_____

_____

Have you ever blamed other people for your actions or decisions when the real culprit is fear? How can you take responsibility for the fear you feel so you can begin to move beyond it?

_____

_____

Take a moment to think, pray, and write about how you would feel and what you would do if fear did not hold you back. What would your life be like if you allowed courage instead of fear to direct your decisions?

_____

_____

Keep This in Mind

God gave us a spirit not of fear but of power and love and self-control.
2 Timothy 1:7 (ESV)

You can choose today to break free from the spirit of fear and to live the rest of your life in faith and power!

PART 1

Understanding Fear

CHAPTER 1

It's Time to Make a Choice

Setting Your Mind on Victory

Basically there are two paths you can walk: faith or fear. It's impossible to simultaneously trust God and not trust God.

Charles Stanley

Why is it impossible to walk in faith and fear at the same time?

_____

_____

_____

How can you choose faith over fear in a specific area of your life this week?

_____

_____

_____

Doing It Afraid

The memory of an incident in LaVondria's childhood caused her to feel afraid years after the incident happened. Is there anything in your past that still provokes fear in you when you think about it today?

_____

_____

LaVondria learned to depend on Philippians 4:6 and 4:13 to help her fight fear. How can these verses help you fight fear, too?

_____

_____

How does LaVondria's story inspire you to choose to fight fear with God's Word?

_____

_____

Fear-Fighting Truths

These are the key truths from chapter 1. Check the ones you most need to believe and apply to your life.

- God has a great plan for your life. The devil also has a plan, and it is not a good one. You can choose God's plan by trusting what He says in His Word, or you can choose the devil's plan by believing his lies. You have the power to choose which plan to follow.
- One way the enemy lies to people is to cause them to think they can make bad choices and still end up with good results.
- God is constantly drawing you toward His will, and His grace is always available to help you make the right choices.
- Allowing fear to dictate your decisions will not only rob you of the good life God has for you, it probably will also affect the people around you in a negative way.
- The way to conquer fear is through faith. Trusting and obeying God completely requires you to have faith.
- God prepares you and provides you with everything you need to follow the path He has prepared for you.
- It is never too late to make the right choice. Make your next choice a good choice!

Taking Courage in the Word

When you read **Deuteronomy 30:19** and think about what choosing life means to you, what comes to mind? What are some specific ways you can choose life and blessings?

_____

_____

What does **John 10:10** say about the way God wants you to live through Jesus Christ? What does the enemy want to do to you?

_____

_____

What can you learn about the enemy from **John 8:44**?

_____

_____

Some people choose the enemy's plan for their lives simply because they are ignorant of his ways. What does **Hosea 4:6** say about a lack of knowledge?

_____

_____

What does **Ephesians 2:10** (AMPC) say you need to do in order to walk in the good life God has prearranged for you?

_____

_____

What do these verses say about sin?
Numbers 32:23 (KJV)

_____

_____

Romans 6:23

_____

_____

Why did Jesus rebuke Peter in **Matthew 14:25–31**? If you have lost your faith in any area of your life, how can you begin to walk in faith again?

_____

_____

What important lessons can you learn from **1 Samuel 13:1–14** and **1 Samuel 15:1–23?**

_____

_____

According to **Matthew 25:21, 23**, why is it important to be trustworthy in little things?

_____

_____

Do you believe God is asking you to be trustworthy in something seemingly insignificant right now? If so, how can you improve in this area?

_____

_____

Moving Forward in Freedom

What is the difference between God's plan for your life and the devil's plan for your life? Which one will you choose?

_____

_____

Fill in the blanks in this statement from the second paragraph of chapter 1: "God has given us free will, which means we can do _____ _____ _____ _____ _____. We have _____, and each one we make brings a _____."

What are some daily choices you may need to make in order to align your life with God's Word?

_____

_____

According to the section "Living the Good Life," why do so many people make wrong choices?

_____

_____

Has anyone close to you ever made fear-based decisions? How did those choices affect your life?

_____

_____

_____

What do you read in the section "Choose Faith" about the way God feels when people choose fear? Why?

_____

_____

Fill in the blanks in these sentences from the section "God Prepares Us for What He Has Planned for Us": "Partial obedience is not _____. It is a little _____ mixed with a lot of _____ and _____, and it doesn't _____."

What are some tests of obedience God has allowed you to face?

_____

_____

_____

In your life right now, how are you making choices to obey God, to choose life and His blessings? Why are they choices you will be happy with later on?

_____

_____

_____

Keep This in Mind

This day I call the heavens and the earth as witnesses against you that I have set before you life and death, blessings and curses. Now choose life, so that you and your children may live.

Deuteronomy 30:19

Whether you walk in faith or in fear is a decision you must make many times throughout your life, sometimes daily. If you make right choices according to God's will, you experience His blessings. But if you choose what you know is wrong, you will face consequences you won't like or enjoy. God's desire is for you to make good choices all the time.

CHAPTER 2

Do It Afraid

Setting Your Mind on Victory

When you are afraid, do the thing you are afraid of and soon you will lose your fear of it.

Norman Vincent Peale

What is "the thing you are afraid of"? Feel free to list more than one.

_____

_____

Why would doing the thing you are afraid of cause you to lose your fear of it?

_____

_____

Doing It Afraid

Carolyn refers to water as her "phobia." Do you have a phobia or a specific intense fear? If so, what is it?

_____

_____

How does Carolyn's story encourage you to believe that no matter your age or how many times you may have tried and failed, you can still experience victory and breakthrough when doing something afraid?

_____

_____

For Carolyn, learning to swim was a lifetime achievement. What fear could you conquer as a lifetime achievement?

_____

_____

Fear-Fighting Truths

These are the key truths from chapter 2. Check the ones you most need to believe and apply to your life.

- Fear can be described as running away from something because of an unpleasant emotion or feeling that you may suffer or be harmed in some way.
- No matter what is happening in your life or in the world around you, God is greater than it is, and He is with you.
- The only way to live in freedom from fear is to confront fear by doing what causes you to be afraid—even when you feel fearful.
- The understanding that you can feel afraid and still move forward will change your life.
- If you understand what fear really is, it will have no power over you.
- Jesus offers you hope in every situation. No matter how fearful you may feel or how long you have been afraid, there's always the potential for positive change.
- The key to courage is simply to keep trying to be courageous day after day, no matter how long it takes.
- Freedom from fear does not mean you never *feel* afraid; it means you do not allow fear to control you or influence your decisions.
- Whether you think your fear is big or small, it's still fear. Be diligent to face even the fears that seem minor.

• Fear will persist for as long as you allow it to affect you. Once you confront it, it must back down.

Taking Courage in the Word

Fill in the blanks in **Joshua 1:9**: "Have I not commanded you? Be _____
_____ and _____. Do not be _____; do not be _____
_____, for the Lord your God will be _____ you wherever you go."
In the following verses, God tells us why we should not fear. What does He
say in each one?
Isaiah 41:10

_____

_____

_____

Isaiah 43:1

_____

_____

Revelation 1:17

_____

_____

What encouraging truths can you learn from these verses?
Romans 8:31

_____

_____

1 John 4:4

_____

_____

What does **1 Peter 1:3** say is one of the blessings of being born again?

_____

_____

_____

According to the last paragraph of chapter 2, what are "flaming arrows of the evil one" (also called "flaming darts" or "fiery darts" in some Bible translations) mentioned in **Ephesians 6:16**, and why is faith a shield against them?

_____

_____

Moving Forward in Freedom

What is fear, according to the first section of chapter 2?

_____

_____

What has fear caused you to run away from? How is *Do It Afraid* helping you gain confidence to confront it?

_____

_____

What is the primary reason you do not need to fear?

_____

_____

You can pray for God to supernaturally take away your fear, but what is a better way to pray?

_____

_____

According to the first section of chapter 2, what is the only way you can live free from fear?

_____

_____

_____

The section "Little Fears and Big Fears" says, "Fear does not always show up just for the big events in your life. It is lurking somewhere all the time, hoping for a chance to jump on board in your life, even if it only causes a vague feeling of dread or doubt." How have you experienced this?

What is a seemingly small fear in your life right now, and how can you confront it before it becomes a big fear? Why is this important?

According to the section "We Don't Have to Live in Fear," what are "evil forebodings"? Why do some people struggle with them? If you have wrestled with them, how can the power of hope help you break free from them?

What kind of expectations do you have, generally speaking: good or bad? What kind of expectations does God want you to have?

How is fear like a nagging back pain? What is the best way to deal with it?

Keep This in Mind

Have I not commanded you? Be strong and courageous. Do not be afraid; do not be discouraged, for the Lord your God will be with you wherever you go.

Joshua 1:9

The fact that you *feel* fear does not mean you have to *live* in fear, allowing it to dictate what you will and won't do or interfering with your ability to enjoy your life. You can choose to face fear with faith. You can feel fear and still do it afraid!

CHAPTER 3

I Will Not Fear

Setting Your Mind on Victory

You can conquer almost any fear if you will only make up your mind to do so. For remember, fear doesn't exist anywhere except in the mind.

Dale Carnegie

What specific fear do you need to make up your mind to conquer?

_____

_____

What does it mean that "fear doesn't exist anywhere except in the mind," and how does knowing this help you?

_____

_____

Doing It Afraid

Ginger was afraid of birds because her father feared them after a traumatic experience with a rooster. Is there anything you are afraid of because a parent or family member feared it? What is it and what is the story behind your relative's fear?

_____

_____

How can you break the power of a family member's fear and keep from passing it along to your children?

_____

_____

Have you ever wrestled with fears that may seem unreasonable, such as Ginger's fear of birds? How does her story teach you to resist wrong thoughts and focus on right thoughts to help you defeat fear?

_____

_____

Fear-Fighting Truths

These are the key truths from chapter 3. Check the ones you most need to believe and apply to your life.

- You may feel fear, but you can resist it, which means you don't let it control you.
- God is always with you. You have never been anywhere that He has not been right there with you, nor will you ever go anywhere without Him. Even if you are not aware of His presence, He is with you all the time.
- You cannot see God's presence with your physical eyes, but He's always available to you. The promise and the reality of His presence will keep you strong through even the most difficult times.
- A specific fear that torments many people, perhaps even you, is the fear of not getting what they want or the fear of missing out on something important to them.
- Fear can manifest in different ways other than what we normally consider being frightened. Worry, dread, nervousness, and even jealousy are also forms of fear and are rooted in fear.
- It's important to practice being aware of God's constant presence, even when distractions tempt you to forget that He is near.

- God wants to be involved in every aspect of your life. Developing an awareness of His presence will help you live with courage and confidence instead of fear.

Taking Courage in the Word

Learning to fill your mind with the truth of God's Word is vital to breaking free from fear. Today, apply **Psalm 118:6** to your life by completing this sentence: Because the Lord is with me, I will not be afraid of _____. Speak this aloud and repeat it as many times as necessary for you to believe it in your heart.

The people mentioned in the following verses all had one promise in common. What is it?

_____

How did that promise affect their lives?
Genesis 6:18

_____

Genesis 17:7, 19 and **Romans 4:17**

_____

Genesis 28:15

_____

Acts 18:10

_____

David writes in **Psalm 23:4**, "Even though I walk through the darkest valley, I will fear no evil, for you are with me." What is the darkest valley (the most frightening, saddest, or most overwhelming circumstance) you have walked through in your life? How did you experience God's presence and faithfulness in those situations? How did God help you fight fear during those times?

_____

_____

In **Matthew 1:23**, Jesus is called "Immanuel," which means "God with us." How have you experienced God's presence in your life, and how do you need His presence in special ways right now?

_____

_____

_____

What does **Jeremiah 29:13** promise you if you will seek God?

_____

_____

_____

What can you learn from **Proverbs 16:9** and **Isaiah 55:8–9** about the difference between the human mind and God's mind?

_____

_____

_____

Jacob says in **Genesis 28:16**, "Surely the Lord is in this place, and I was not aware of it." As you look back through your life, when has God been with you and you were not aware of it? How does this encourage you about your life today and in the future?

_____

_____

_____

Based on **Luke 10:38–42**, what is the most important thing you can do? How can you learn to work *with* Jesus instead of letting your responsibilities, activities, and worries distract you *from* Him?

_____

_____

John 15:5 teaches that abiding in Christ is very important. Why?

_____

_____

Moving Forward in Freedom

According to the first paragraph of chapter 3, what is the only acceptable attitude for a Christian to have toward fear?

_____

_____

Fill in the blanks in this sentence from the last paragraph of the first section of chapter 3: "When we realize that _____ is _____ _____, then and only then will we be _____ _____ _____."
The first paragraph of the section titled "Distractions" teaches that fear will creep into your life when what happens?

_____

_____

Why does the idea that jealousy is often related to fear make sense? Is there a situation in your life or in the life of someone you love where you have seen jealousy at work and now realize it was rooted in fear?

_____

_____

How has the fear of not getting what you want caused a problem for you, or how have you witnessed it causing trouble for someone else? How can you confront and deal with this fear?

_____

_____

What kinds of useless things steal your time with God and distract you from His presence? How can you train yourself to be more focused when you pray?

_____

_____

_____

Has God done anything for you for which you have forgotten to thank Him, as the lepers in the story in Luke 17:11–19 did? Why not take time to thank Him right now?

Before you go to bed tonight, take a few minutes to review your day and notice ways God was with you even though you weren't aware of it at the time. Thank Him for never leaving you and for being involved in every aspect of your life.

Keep This in Mind

The Lord is with me; I will not be afraid.

Psalm 118:6

God is never more than a thought away. Think about Him and talk to Him throughout the day. Recognizing His presence will give you courage and confidence rather than fear.

CHAPTER 4

Fearful Thoughts and Words

Setting Your Mind on Victory

Fear defeats more people than any other one thing in the world.

Ralph Waldo Emerson

How has fear been an instrument of defeat in your life?

_____

_____

In what areas has fear gained victory over you, and how can you begin to defeat it instead?

_____

_____

Doing It Afraid

Does Rachael's story bring to mind anything about which you have spoken fear-filled words instead of faith-filled ones? Is there something in your life right now about which you need to stop speaking fear and begin to speak faith?

_____

_____

What fearful patterns characterize your speech about certain things, and how can you change your words to reflect faith instead?

_____

_____

_____

Fear-Fighting Truths

These are the key truths from chapter 4. Check the ones you most need to believe and apply to your life.

- Before your life can change, your mind needs to change. When you learn to think differently, you begin to live differently.
- Your mind is a battlefield. It's where the enemy attacks you with thoughts that are not true and tries to get you to believe them. If he can do that, he can make you miserable. That's why aligning your thoughts with God's Word is vital.
- Renewing the mind is a process. It doesn't happen overnight, and it requires effort. With God's help, you can do it!
- You do not have to focus on any thought that enters your mind. You can choose what you think about, rejecting unbiblical thoughts from the enemy and embracing thoughts that are in agreement with God's character and His Word.
- A good way to grow in faith is to begin to imagine and pray for things that are impossible to you but are possible with God and that reflect His will for your life, according to His Word. Then do your part, with God's help, to work to see those things become realities.
- The thoughts and attitudes you allow in your mind become the words you speak and, ultimately, the actions you take and behaviors you display. They actually shape and determine the way you will live.

Taking Courage in the Word

Read **Romans 12:2**. How does the renewing of your mind transform you and empower you to live according to God's will?

_____

_____

_____

Based on **John 8:32**, if you continue in the truth, which is God's Word, and obey it, what will it produce in your life?

_____

_____

_____

According to **Colossians 3:2** (AMPC), what should you continually think about?

_____

_____

_____

How does **2 Corinthians 10:4–6** teach you to handle your thoughts?

_____

_____

What does **Proverbs 23:7** indicate about how powerful thoughts are?

_____

_____

What does **Matthew 12:34** say about the relationship between what we think or feel and what we speak?

_____

_____

What can you learn in the section "Thoughts Become Words, Attitudes, and Actions" from **Proverbs 18:20–21** and **James 3:2–10**?

_____

_____

Moving Forward in Freedom

Identifying wrong beliefs (beliefs that are not in agreement with God's Word) and replacing them with right ones (beliefs that align with God's Word) is a key to breaking free from fear. What wrong beliefs have you held—or do you hold—that do not reflect the truth of God's Word?

_____

_____

How can you break the power of the wrong beliefs by applying biblical truth to them? You may wish to use a concordance or an Internet search to help you find Bible verses or passages on the subjects you have identified. For example, if you believe people do not accept you, look for scriptures on God's love and acceptance, or if you believe you can never break free from fear or anxiety, look for scriptures on overcoming fear and anxiety and finding peace.

_____

_____

What does it mean to be deceived?

_____

_____

What is a stronghold, and how are strongholds built in our minds?

_____

_____

What are some thoughts you can think on purpose in order to do something afraid? Examples include *I can do whatever I need to do in life through Christ who is my strength* (based on Philippians 4:13) and *I love people, and I love to give and be generous.*

_____

_____

To walk strong in God, we need to be in agreement with Him (Amos 3:3). Are your thoughts and imaginings in agreement with God and based on His Word? If not, what can you do to change this?

_____

_____

How have you seen thoughts lead to words, which lead to certain attitudes, which then lead to actions in your life or in the life of someone else?

_____

_____

Keep This in Mind

For as he thinks in his heart, so is he.

Proverbs 23:7 AMPC

The tongue has the power of life and death, and those who love it will eat its fruit.

Proverbs 18:21

If your thoughts and words are rooted in fear, you will prevent yourself from making progress in life. Thoughts and words are so powerful that they can either imprison you or set you free. Instead of thinking and saying, "I'm afraid," learn to think and speak, "When I feel fear, I will do it afraid."

CHAPTER 5

I "Feel" Afraid

Setting Your Mind on Victory

Don't pray for tasks equal to your powers. Pray for power equal to your tasks.

Phillips Brooks

Have you prayed about your fear, or have you simply wished it would go away? Take time today to ask God to set you free from fear and give you the power to do and be everything He desires for you to accomplish and become.

Doing It Afraid

Shawn was delivered from forty years of debilitating fear by facing those fears one step at a time, taking on challenges of increasing difficulty. What do you consider your most debilitating fear?

_____

_____

How does your greatest fear keep you from doing what you want to do, answering God's call, or simply enjoying life?

_____

_____

How does Shawn's story encourage you to face a particular fear in your life by gradually doing certain things afraid until you can finally conquer your most significant fear?

Fear-Fighting Truths

These are the key truths from chapter 5. Check the ones you most need to believe and apply to your life.

- The feeling of fear is real. It is such a powerful emotion that it can produce physical symptoms.
- If you allow it to do so, fear will steal from you and keep you from doing things that would be fulfilling for you. The better you understand that fear is nothing more than a feeling, the better you can fight and defeat it.
- Doing something afraid can change the course of your entire life.
- Feelings are fickle, unpredictable, and undependable. They are not firm and solid; they can change in an instant.
- The fact that feelings change and are unpredictable is why it is so important to learn to live beyond your feelings and not to allow them to determine whether or not you keep your commitments or the way you live your life.
- The feeling of excitement and the emotion of enthusiasm may influence you to make a commitment and start something, but feelings will rarely carry you all the way through to accomplish a goal.
- Learn to keep your word and to finish what you start.

Taking Courage in the Word

Read **Psalm 56:3**. As a believer in Christ, you are encouraged to say with the psalmist, "When I am afraid, I put my trust in you." If you are struggling with this, ask God to help you trust Him more and more, every time you are afraid.

According to **Ephesians 2:10**, what has God arranged for you? How does this truth give you hope and courage?

What does **Psalm 15:4** say about keeping your word?

According to **Acts 20:24** (AMPC), what was one of the apostle Paul's primary goals? Why should this be one of your goals, too?

What can you learn about Jesus from **John 17:4** and **Hebrews 12:2**?

Moving Forward in Freedom

What, if any, physical manifestations of fear have you experienced?

Have you ever allowed one bad experience to cause you to be afraid of trying something again? What happened, and will you choose today to do it afraid?

In what ways has fear stolen from you?

As you go through life, you may realize you have fears you have not been aware of. According to the first section of chapter 5, why does God not reveal all of our fears at once, and how does that show us His commitment to see us break free from them?

_____

_____

In your life, what experience has taught you how fickle feelings can be?

_____

_____

What does the fact that fear is a feeling and feelings are fickle teach you about fear?

_____

_____

How have you allowed fear and other feelings to dictate or direct certain choices you have made? How can you stop letting your feelings determine your choices?

_____

_____

On a scale of 1–10, with 1 being "not well at all" and 10 being "extremely well," how well do you keep the commitments you make?

_____

What commitments can you choose to honor in your life right now, even though you may not really feel like following through with them?

_____

_____

Keep This in Mind

When I am afraid, I put my trust in you.

Psalm 56:3

Depending on the specific fears people face, they may look to paychecks, medical tests, weather reports, relationships, job opportunities, or other sources to relieve their fears. Remember, fear is simply a feeling, and when you feel afraid, you can choose to put your trust in God.

CHAPTER 6
Why Am I Afraid?

Setting Your Mind on Victory

Of all the liars in the world, sometimes the worst are our own fears.
Rudyard Kipling

One way a fear will lie to you is to say, "You could never..." or "You will always..." These lies are designed to keep you from experiencing all God has for you. In what ways have your fears lied to you?

_____

_____

Why can your own fear sometimes be the worst liar of all?

_____

_____

Doing It Afraid

The fact that tigers paralyze their prey by causing them to be afraid is fascinating. That's exactly what the enemy does to us. In what ways has the fear of what might happen—or the fear of what might not happen—paralyzed you?

_____

_____

_____

The tiger's roar lets out sound at a frequency too low to be heard, but it can be felt. Is there some kind of fear in your life right now that may not manifest outwardly but you can feel it and it has you stuck in a place where the enemy can attack you?

_____

_____

_____

Fear-Fighting Truths

These are the key truths from chapter 6. Check the ones you most need to believe and apply to your life.

- You cannot see the enemy with your natural eyes, but he is real. He is an evil spiritual force, and you can see and feel evidence of his working against you. Many problems and fears have their roots in the enemy and his activities.
- You can resist the enemy by refusing to take the actions fear tries to force you to take, and you can conquer fear by confronting it.
- God has given to every believer power and authority over the enemy, but these gifts work only if you exercise them. You exercise them when you recognize and resist the enemy, counter his lies with the truth of God's Word, and refuse to do what he tempts you to do.
- A reverential fear of God will keep you on the right path in life and prevent you from thinking that disobeying Him does not really matter. God offers forgiveness for sin, but He also requires obedience. Our goal is to choose the path of righteousness.
- The only right kind of fear is the reverential fear of the Lord. In addition, certain other fears may be regarded as "good," such as healthy fears that are based on wisdom and will help you stay safe or ensure your well-being and the protection of the people you love.

- The enemy may hurt you in a certain way, but you can keep him from continuing to hurt you by trapping you in a victim mentality. In Christ you are a victor, not a victim!

- You can choose to put up with fear and allow it to control you, but God has something much better for you! Confront your fear and move into God's wonderful plan for your life—a plan of peace, strength, and victory.

Taking Courage in the Word

According to **John 10:10**, what are the three ways the enemy works to harm you?

_____

_____

Read **Ephesians 4:26–27**. What does it mean to give the enemy a foothold? In what ways might you have allowed him to take advantage of you?

_____

_____

Second Timothy 1:7 says that fear does not come from God. Where does it come from?

_____

_____

Based on **James 4:7**, how can you get the devil to flee from you? What can happen if you don't resist him?

_____

_____

Read **Matthew 16:23**. What does this teach you about the way Satan operates through people?

_____

_____

Fear may say to you, "You cannot do that." **Philippians 4:13** (NKJV) offers the perfect response. What does it say, and how does it encourage you?

_____

_____

What did God say to Joshua in **Joshua 1:5** and **Joshua 1:9**? These verses are as much for you as they were for Joshua!

_____

_____

Read **Luke 4:1–10**. How did Jesus answer Satan every time he lied to Him? Based on Jesus' example in this passage, what is the best way for you to confront the enemy's lies?

_____

_____

_____

Based on **Proverbs 9:10**, what is the beginning of wisdom?

_____

_____

According to **2 Corinthians 5:17**, who are you once you become a Christian? What happens to all the old things about you?

_____

_____

Fill in the blank: According to **Romans 8:37**, you are _____.

Moving Forward in Freedom

Have you ever blamed a situation on another person, your circumstances, or even God and then realized the enemy was at work? How did you come to that realization?

_____

_____

How does the enemy use fear to take advantage of you?

_____

_____

What can you do to more actively resist the enemy's efforts to take advantage of you?

_____

_____

Based on the section "Conquer through Confrontation," what happens when evil is not confronted?

_____

_____

According to the section "Every Believer Has Authority over Satan," "The only right kind of fear is the _____ fear ____ _____, which is an awe-inspiring, _____ type of fear that gives Him _____ above all else."

The reverential fear of the Lord will keep us from treating disobedience to God lightly. Why is it important that we take disobedience seriously?

_____

_____

In what ways are you tempted to live with a victim mentality? How can you break free from that way of thinking?

_____

_____

What are some ways you can give place to the enemy or allow him access to your life?

_____

_____

Why do believers have no right to feel sorry for themselves?

_____

_____

Are you experiencing the torment that often accompanies fear? How would you describe it, and how can you break free from it?

_____

_____

Keep This in Mind

Be alert and of sober mind. Your enemy the devil prowls around like a roaring lion looking for someone to devour.

1 Peter 5:8

Fear is a work of the enemy. Watch out for it and recognize it as something that does not come from God. Resist any temptation to merely put up with it, because it will ultimately control you. The enemy wants to keep you trapped in fear, but God wants to bless you, and He wants you to have great peace and joy.

CHAPTER 7

The Antidote for Fear

Setting Your Mind on Victory

Resist your fear; fear will never lead you to a positive end. Go for your faith and what you believe.

T. D. Jakes

What are some effective ways you are learning to resist fear through this study?

_____

_____

Fear never leads to a positive outcome, but faith always does. How have you experienced fear leading you in a negative direction and faith leading you to a positive end?

_____

_____

Doing It Afraid

Like Donna, have you ever struggled with a fear that has tormented you for as long as you can remember, one you never outgrew? How can a closer relationship with God help you confront that fear?

_____

_____

Donna discovered that God had not left her alone to face her fears and realized that He was with her to help her conquer them. In what situations do you need to trust that God is always with you and ask Him to help you overcome every fear you face?

_____

_____

The Lord led Donna to memorize scriptures about fear, which helped her defeat it. What scriptures will you choose to memorize to help you overcome fear? You can find many verses to memorize throughout *Do It Afraid*.

_____

Fear-Fighting Truths

These are the key truths from chapter 7. Check the ones you most need to believe and apply to your life.

- One reason you can live without fear is that God loves you with a perfect love. You can be confident in His love all the time, in every circumstance.
- Insecurity and feelings of inadequacy are forms of fear. The way to break free from them is to believe in your heart that God loves you and to receive and live with confidence in His love.
- God's love is being poured out on you all the time. It is a gift, which you can never earn nor deserve. You receive it by faith, knowing that God loves you so much that He sent His only Son to die for your sins and reconcile you to Himself.
- Bouncing between feeling proud of yourself when you think you have done well and feeling guilty when you think you haven't will waste your time and energy. Your performance does not change God's love for you.
- Your relationship with yourself is vitally important. Do whatever you need to do to make sure your relationship with yourself is strong and healthy and to love yourself in a godly way.

- Fear and insecurity will not willingly let you go. Choose to be aggressive against them so you can be free to become all God wants you to be and enjoy the life He wants you to live.

Taking Courage in the Word

According to **1 John 4:18**, what is the antidote to fear?

_____

Read **Romans 8:35, 37–39**. What can you learn from this passage and how does it encourage you?

_____

_____

_____

Based on **Romans 5:5**, where can you find the love of God?

_____

_____

_____

Read **Romans 5:6–8** and **Ephesians 2:4–5**. What do these passages teach you about Christ's love and the fact that people can never deserve it?

_____

_____

According to **Psalm 40:2** (ESV), what does God do for those who feel they are in "the pit of destruction"?

_____

Read **Luke 22:54–62** and **Acts 2:41**. How did Peter behave in Luke 22? After the Holy Spirit touched him, how did Peter's ministry affect people in Acts 2? Do you believe God can work a similar transformation in you?

_____

_____

Fill in the blanks: **Ephesians 6:10** (ESV) encourages you to "Be _____ in the Lord and in the _____ ____ _____ _____."

Moving Forward in Freedom

What is "the cure for the insecure"?

_____

Do you have a healthy relationship with yourself? If not, how can you receive God's love and begin to love yourself in a balanced way, as God loves you? Why is this important?

_____

_____

_____

God made you unique and special, and He loves you just as you are. What are some of your unique characteristics or abilities? What are your best qualities?

_____

_____

_____

When we love God, we want to obey Him. How can you be obedient to God this week as a way of demonstrating your love for Him?

_____

_____

_____

Why is it extremely difficult to be set free from something if we refuse to admit that it is a problem or if we use it as a means to control other people?

_____

_____

Fill in the blanks: The third paragraph of the section "Secure in Christ" says that God "is an expert at _____ the brokenhearted and making the _____ _____."

What practical steps can you take to be aggressive against fear and insecurity so you will become everything God wants you to be?

_____

_____

Keep This in Mind

There is no fear in love. But perfect love drives out fear, because fear has to do with punishment. The one who fears is not made perfect in love.

1 John 4:18

God's love is not given in varying degrees based on our level of so-called perfection. God is love! He loves us because He is kind and He wants to love us. No matter what you do, it won't stop God from loving you. It may stop you from receiving His love, but His love is always present to heal and deliver—no matter what.

Living Boldly

Setting Your Mind on Victory

The brave man is not he who does not feel afraid, but he who conquers that fear.

Nelson Mandela

Popular opinion might say the brave person is one who doesn't feel afraid. Why is that not true?

_____

_____

Nelson Mandela's quotation summarizes the message of doing it afraid and reminds us that courage lies in conquering our fears even when we feel afraid. How is the material in *Do It Afraid* teaching you to do things even when you feel fear?

_____

_____

_____

Doing It Afraid

Have you, like Melanie, ever felt confident doing something for years and then found yourself afraid to do it later in life? How did that affect you?

Consider the last paragraph of Melanie's story, and think about how facing her fear truly transformed her life: "I can honestly say that I'm not the
woman I used to be. I am bolder, more confident, and more apt to try new
things. And it all began when I decided to do it afraid—and sing." Your greatest breakthrough may be just on the other side of your greatest fear. What is
your greatest fear, and what step could you take toward confronting it?

Fear-Fighting Truths

These are the key truths from chapter 8. Check the ones you most need to
believe and apply to your life.

- God has more than enough of everything you could ever need.
- When faced with a new challenge or opportunity, don't ask yourself if
  you can do it in your own strength. Ask God if He can do it through you.
- You can do anything God asks you to do, as long as you rely on Him.
- Faith leads to boldness, and boldness leads to success.
- Until we realize that God's power—not human strength—works through
  us, we will limit ourselves to only what we feel capable of doing.
- When you face a difficult situation, receive God's grace by faith and rely
  on it to see you through your hard times. When you feel weak or unable
  to deal with something, know that God's grace will carry you through it.
- Extraordinary power is available to you in Christ. Once you truly realize that He offers you this kind of power, you will no longer allow fear to
  dictate your decisions or rule your life.
- There are at least three ways to short-circuit God's power in your life:
  complaining, self-pity, and being greedy for glory.

Taking Courage in the Word

Read **Proverbs 28:1**. Do you view yourself as righteous? What can you learn about your righteousness from these Bible verses?

Romans 3:21–22

_____

Romans 10:4

_____

2 Corinthians 5:21

_____

Philippians 3:8–9

_____

Chapter 8 is a chapter that builds faith. How do the following scriptures help you grow in your faith and trust in God?

Job 36:26

_____

Luke 18:27

_____

1 Corinthians 2:9 (AMPC)

_____

Read **Matthew 14:25–33** and **Joshua 3:5–17**. How do these stories encourage you, and what do they teach you about faith and boldness?

_____

_____

_____

In **Ephesians 1:18–19**, what did Paul pray that the believers at Ephesus would understand? You can pray for this same understanding!

_____

According to **Ephesians 3:20**, what is God able to do through His power that works in us? Please notice that the scripture says God does it _through_ His power working _in_ us. God doesn't do it _for_ us.

_____

_____

Based on **James 4:6**, you can believe that when God gives grace and you need more of it, He will give you _____ _____.

Ephesians 2:8 teaches that salvation comes by _____ through _____.

According to **Colossians 1:4** (AMPC), what is faith?

_____

_____

Matthew 11:28 assures us that Jesus offers us rest. It is not rest *from* work, but rest *while* we work. How can you experience that in a practical way?

_____

_____

What does **Psalm 100:4** teach you to do?

_____

_____

What can you learn *not* to do from **Philippians 2:12–14**?

_____

_____

Read **Daniel 1:8** and **6:16–23**. What lessons about power, faith, and gratitude does this story offer?

_____

_____

What do these verses say about being careful not to try to take the glory of God?

Isaiah 48:11

_____

1 Corinthians 1:29

_____

Psalm 36:11 (AMPC)

_____

Moving Forward in Freedom

In what areas of your life do you need to resist the temptation to ask, "Do I think I can do this?" and instead ask, "God, can You do this?"

_____

_____

Chapter 8 of *Do It Afraid* says: "I can assure you that you can do anything that God asks you to do, no matter how difficult it is or how much experience you lack, if you will keep your eyes on Him and realize He is more than enough." When you read these words, what comes to mind for you? What is God asking you to do, and will you choose to believe that He is more than enough?

_____

_____

How can the enemy, through fear, steal the blessings God has for you when you need to do something afraid?

_____

_____

See the second paragraph of the section "How Do They Do It?" and fill in the blanks: "Grace is _____, _____, and _____ _____. It is God doing something for us or helping us when we do not _____ it. Grace is _____, God's favor, and the _____ of the Holy Spirit to meet our _____ and _____."

Why is it foolish to try to do things in your own strength? How could your life improve if you were to allow God's power to flow through you instead of striving to make things happen on your own?

_____

_____

How will you keep yourself connected to God's power over the next week?

_____

_____

Complaining is one way believers can short-circuit the flow of God's power in their lives. What situation in your life have you been tempted to complain about, and how can you express gratitude to God instead?

_____

_____

Christians can short-circuit God's power flowing through their lives through self-pity. How can you move away from self-pity and cultivate a healthier, more positive attitude?

_____

_____

When a believer is greedy for the glory (or credit) that belongs to God, that attitude short-circuits God's power in that person's life. Why?

_____

_____

What are some practical ways you can stay plugged in to God, your power source?

_____

_____

Keep This in Mind

The wicked flee though no one pursues, but the righteous are as bold as a lion.

Proverbs 28:1

Peter had to get out of the boat in order to walk on water (Matt. 14:29). Joshua and the priests had to put their feet in the Jordan River before the waters parted (Josh. 3:5–17). And you and I will often have to take steps of action while we feel afraid. God gives us the boldness we need to do what He calls us to do.

PART 2

Confronting Fear

CHAPTER 9

Take One Step at a Time

Setting Your Mind on Victory

Faith is taking the first step even when you don't see the whole staircase.
                                        Martin Luther King Jr.

Are you trying to see the "whole staircase" in an area of your life? In other words, do you want God to show you everything about a certain situation before you are willing to begin to move forward?

_____

_____

_____

How can you move ahead this week—just a little bit—trusting God even though you cannot see as much as you would like to see?

_____

_____

Doing It Afraid

Michele writes about flying as a young person and experiencing panic, having her eyes well up with tears and struggling to catch her breath. Have you ever had fear manifest itself in physical ways? Name the fear and describe your reaction to it.

Michele came to realize that God would not force her to face her fear of flying, but that she needed to choose to take the first step toward her breakthrough. What is one step you can take this week toward breaking through the power fear has had in your life?

Fear-Fighting Truths

These are the key truths from chapter 9. Check the ones you most need to believe and apply to your life.

- The best way to conquer fear is to focus on taking one step at a time instead of thinking about all the steps you will need to take eventually.
- God gives grace for one step at a time. Moving forward step by step enables you to gradually develop a firm, solid trust in Him.
- Never underestimate the power of little victories on a regular basis.
- Starting a journey to freedom in any area of life is easy, but finishing requires a commitment to continue, even when facing challenges.
- Becoming a victorious Christian is similar to succeeding in other ways. It requires time, energy, focus, dedication, and perseverance.
- Freedom must first be gained and then maintained. The key to gaining freedom is the same as the key to maintaining it: making right choices in little ways day by day.
- God is looking for you to take a step in the right direction. Take the first step, and you will find grace to take the next one.
- Don't put yourself on a schedule for your breakthrough; just keep trying and keep moving forward, no matter how long it takes.

- The only way you can fail at something is to quit trying. As long as you're making an effort, you're moving forward.

Taking Courage in the Word

Read **Psalm 37:23**. Have you ever taken a step that seemed shaky before you took it, only to realize that God had set your feet in a firm place? What was the step, and how did you realize that it was solid and stable?

_____

_____

What can you learn about the journey to freedom from fear or freedom in any area of your life from **Deuteronomy 7:22**?

_____

_____

Depending on the version of the Bible you read, Jesus says in **John 8:31** to "hold to" or to "abide" in His Word (His teaching), which carries the same meaning as "to continue" in it. What is God's promise for those who do continue in it, according to **John 8:32**?

_____

_____

The apostle Paul taught about the importance of continuing. In these verses, what are the specific ways in which he urged his readers to continue, and why is this instruction also important for you?
Colossians 4:2–6

_____

2 Timothy 3:14

_____

Galatians 5:1 (In this verse, the idea of continuing is represented in some translations by the words _stand firm_ or _stand fast_.)

_____

_____

Moving Forward in Freedom

As you read *Do It Afraid,* what specific fear(s) come to mind that you would like to conquer? If you're feeling hesitant or overwhelmed to take a step, how can you do it afraid?

_____

_____

How has fear controlled aspects of your life?

_____

_____

According to the first section of chapter 9, what is a better way to pray than simply asking God to take away your fear?

_____

_____

Why is the idea of *continuing* so vital to breaking free from fear and to pursuing any other breakthrough you may need?

_____

_____

_____

Fill in the blanks in these sentences from the second-to-last paragraph in the section titled "Continue": "Paul was well aware that freedom first had to be _____ and then _____. He knew it was not a onetime event, but a _____ commitment of _____ to do what was right day after day after day."
Why is thinking about an entire journey all at once discouraging? Why is it better to think of it one step at a time?

_____

_____

How does the story about exercise and working with a personal trainer inspire you to do what you can do when you can do it and reinforce the importance of moving toward a goal step by step?

In what area of your life do you need to take the first step toward freedom and/or greater strength?

What may be holding you back from taking that first step, and how can you overcome that hindrance?

Keep This in Mind

The Lord your God will drive out those nations before you, little by little. You will not be allowed to eliminate them all at once, or the wild animals will multiply around you.

Deuteronomy 7:22

If some type of fear is holding you back from fulfilling your destiny or obeying God, don't make excuses for it or simply put up with it for the rest of your life. Take one step to conquer it, and then another and another, and don't give up until you arrive at complete freedom, no matter how long it takes. You never fail as long as you keep trying!

CHAPTER 10

Stand Up to Doubt and Double-Mindedness

Setting Your Mind on Victory

Inaction breeds doubt and fear. Action breeds confidence and courage. If you want to conquer fear, do not sit home and think about it. Go out and get busy.

Dale Carnegie

Why does inaction breed doubt and fear, and why does action breed confidence and courage?

_____

_____

Why does getting busy help you conquer fear?

_____

_____

Doing It Afraid

When illness threatened Cindy's longtime dream of singing professionally, which she also believed to be God's call on her life, she struggled with doubt. What has caused you to wrestle with doubt?

_____

_____

Even though Cindy went through a season of doubt about her voice, God brought it back stronger than it was before her illness. How does her experience help build your faith?

_____

_____

_____

Fear-Fighting Truths

These are the key truths from chapter 10. Check the ones you most need to believe and apply to your life.

- Doubt does not manifest as other types of fear do, but it is still a form of fear, and it will steal your faith.
- To truly live free from fear, you also need to resist all forms of doubt.
- The enemy launches attacks of doubt against everyone, so don't feel condemned if you struggle or have struggled with doubt. Learn to recognize it for what it is: the enemy's sneaky attempt to bring fear into your life.
- Of all the types of doubt, self-doubt is perhaps the most tormenting.
- Sometimes the only way to stop doubting is to make a decision. If that decision is not right or good, God can redeem it.
- God wants you to be able to trust Him without doubting and to be confident that you hear His voice.
- If you want to hear God's voice and be led by Him, start by believing you can and do hear Him.
- Self-doubt and double-mindedness are often rooted in the fear of being wrong. It's important to realize that being wrong about something or making wrong decisions doesn't make you wrong as a person.
- Everyone makes mistakes. One way to handle them is to ask God to use them for good. Another way is to admit the mistake and move on instead of dwelling on it.

Taking Courage in the Word

Read **Luke 24:38**. If you were to answer the question Jesus asks in this verse, what would you say? What troubles you and causes you to doubt?

_____

_____

According to **Romans 4:20** (AMPC), what was Abraham's attitude as he waited on God to work a miracle? Do you think it would have been easy for him to doubt?

_____

_____

How does **Ephesians 3:20** describe God's ability to work on your behalf when you trust Him?

_____

_____

Fill in the blanks in **James 1:6–8**: "But when you ask, you must _____ and not _____, because the one who _____ is like a wave of the sea, _____ and _____ by the wind. That person should not expect to receive _____ from the Lord. Such a person is _____ _____ and _____ in all they do."

How does **Romans 8:28** comfort you when you think about mistakes you have made or may make in the future?

_____

_____

What does **1 Corinthians 2:16** say about your mind?

_____

_____

What does **John 14:17** say about the Holy Spirit? Why is this encouraging?

_____

_____

Read **Romans 8:31**. How does this verse give you hope?

Moving Forward in Freedom

Have you ever thought about doubt as a subtle form of fear? Why is it a form of fear?

_____

_____

Fill in the blanks in this sentence from the first section of chapter 10: "God wants us to have _____ _____ in Him, but Satan wants our lives to be _____ by a variety of _____ manifesting in different ways."

According to the first section of chapter 10, what does *doubt* mean?

_____

_____

Chapter 10 includes a list of thoughts that are common when people experience self-doubt. Check the ones that apply to you, then write ways you can think differently, knowing that the enemy wants you to waste your energy rehearsing what you should or should not have done, while God wants to help you move forward.

- I shouldn't have done that!
- I shouldn't have said that!
- I shouldn't have bought that!
- I shouldn't have gone there!
- I shouldn't have eaten that!
- I didn't pray long enough or the right way!
- I spent too much at the grocery store!
- I talk too much!
- I should be quieter!

- I should have spoken up!
- I should be a better parent!
- I have trouble making decisions!

If you want to hear from God and be led by the Holy Spirit, how do you begin?

_____

_____

_____

On a scale of 1–10, with 1 being "almost always" and 10 being "almost never," how frequently do you doubt the decisions you make? What are you learning from chapter 10 about making decisions and sticking with them?

_____

_____

_____

How does the story of the father who tells his children to "go play" illustrate the way God may feel about the decisions you make?

_____

_____

_____

According to the section "The Fear of Being Wrong," why should you not fear being wrong?

_____

_____

What are some positive ways to handle mistakes?

_____

_____

Fill in the blanks in this sentence from the section "The Fear of Being Wrong": "When you need to make a decision, _____ about it, _____ over your options, consider the _____ _____ _____ of each way you could go, and then _____ make a decision."

Keep This in Mind

He said to them, "Why are you troubled, and why do doubts rise in your minds?"

Luke 24:38

God is for you, so it really doesn't matter who is against you or what people think (Rom. 8:31). Live boldly for God and enjoy the life He has given you. Don't let doubt and double-mindedness steal your peace and joy.

CHAPTER 11

Refuse to Regret the Past or Dread the Future

Setting Your Mind on Victory

Gratitude looks to the past and love to the present; fear, avarice, lust, and ambition look ahead.

C. S. Lewis, *The Screwtape Letters*

Why does gratitude look to the past?

_____

_____

How does love operate in the present?

_____

_____

_____

What would be a better way to look toward the future than with fear?

_____

_____

Doing It Afraid

Various uncertainties caused Sophie to fear during her cheerleading tryouts, so she did not complete them the first day. Have you ever allowed unexpected circumstances to make you afraid to do something you wanted to do?

Prayer and the decision to "do it afraid" empowered Sophie to press through her fear. How can prayer and moving forward in the face of fear help you in a situation you are currently facing?

Fear-Fighting Truths

These are the key truths from chapter 11. Check the ones you most need to believe and apply to your life.

- If you choose to dwell on the past or focus on your hopes and plans for the future, you will miss what God has for you in the present. The greatest moment in your life is the one you have right now.
- You cannot change your past, but you can ask God to redeem it or "recycle" it and use it for something good.
- Your history is not your destiny.
- Decide today that you will not spend any more of your life regretting the past, but that you will embrace today with joy and look toward tomorrow with hope.
- Hope motivates you to get up each morning believing that God is good and He has a good plan for your life.
- When you choose to trust God, you're also choosing to live with some unanswered questions.
- Don't miss the good that God has for you today by regretting what happened yesterday.
- Dread is a type of fear. The way to defeat it is to pray immediately when you begin to dread something and ask God to give you the grace to do it with a good attitude.

- If you want to be happy, don't live in regret over the past or in fear of the future.

Taking Courage in the Word

Read **Exodus 3:14** and **Matthew 14:27** (AMPC). What does it mean to you that God does not call Himself "I was" or "I will be," but that He refers to Himself as "I AM"?

_____

_____

Fill in the blanks in **Isaiah 43:18–19**: "_____ the former things; do not dwell on the _____. See, I am doing a _____ thing! Now it springs up; do you not perceive it? I am _____ ___ _____ in the wilderness and streams in the wasteland."

What can you learn about the past from **2 Corinthians 5:17**?

_____

_____

_____

What do these verses teach you about the fact that God is willing and able to give you a fresh start?

Lamentations 3:22–23

_____

_____

Philippians 3:13–14

_____

_____

Isaiah 65:17

_____

_____

What does it mean to you to have a personal relationship with Christ and to be born again "into a living hope," as **1 Peter 1:3** says?

How does **Colossians 3:23** help you fight dread?

How do **Proverbs 16:9** and **27:23** encourage you to plan wisely for the future while also trusting God?

How does **Ecclesiastes 5:1** (AMPC) encourage you to live in the present?

Moving Forward in Freedom

How do you typically handle mistakes? After reading chapter 10, how will you deal differently with the mistakes you will make in the future?

How have you seen God redeem your past? What areas of your past are you still asking and believing for Him to redeem?

In what ways has the enemy lied to you to try to make you believe your history is your destiny?

What is the definition of hope, according to the section "The Power of Hope"?

How can you heed Robert Schuller's advice to "Let your hopes, not your hurts, shape your future"?

_____

_____

Why is it so important to live in hope?

_____

_____

How are you experiencing the power of hope in your life right now? In what areas of your life does your hope need to grow stronger?

_____

_____

Trust requires unanswered questions. What are you trusting God for, and how are you demonstrating your trust in Him?

_____

_____

What is the only day you are assured of, and how can you make the most of it?

_____

_____

What are some ways you are tempted to waste the present moment God has given you?

_____

_____

_____

How can you embrace the present instead of wasting it?

_____

_____

Dread is a form of fear. What do you dread most? What is the best strategy for defeating dread?

_____

_____

Keep This in Mind

This is the day the Lord has made; we will rejoice and be glad in it.
Psalm 118:24 (NKJV)

If you want to be happy and free from fear and regret, don't dwell on the past or worry about the future. Remember that your history is not your destiny, focus on living fully in the present, and trust God for your future.

Take Courage and Be Strong

Setting Your Mind on Victory

One of the greatest discoveries a man makes, one of his great surprises,
is to find he can do what he was afraid he couldn't do.

Henry Ford

Why is it a great discovery and a great surprise to find out you can do something you were afraid you couldn't do?

_____

_____

What have you discovered you can do that you once feared you could not do?

_____

_____

_____

What do you hope to do in the future that you may be afraid of doing now?

_____

_____

Doing It Afraid

Megan struggled with an intense fear of being alone. Have you ever felt this particular fear? How might you be experiencing it currently?

_____

_____

How did God prepare Megan to face her fear and, over time, make tremendous progress toward conquering it?

_____

_____

As God prepares you to confront and overcome your fears, how will you take small steps toward victory, as Megan did, and allow Him to set you free little by little?

_____

_____

Fear-Fighting Truths

These are the key truths from chapter 12. Check the ones you most need to believe and apply to your life.

- Courage is always available, but you have to choose to take it if you want it to work for you. When you are filled with courage, there's no room for fear in your life.
- Instead of simply praying to overcome your fear, pray that God will fill you with boldness, confidence, and courage.
- You may feel fear and courage at the same time. When you do, focus on courage so that it will become the strongest factor in your situation. The more you focus on it, the more you will walk in it.
- Instead of thinking about what you are afraid of, think about who God is.
- You can gain great strength from simply being encouraged. The Holy Spirit lives in you and will strengthen you and encourage you in all the things you need to do.

- It is not only important for you to receive encouragement from the Holy Spirit, it's also important for you to extend the ministry of encouragement to others.
- One of the best things you can do is to meditate on God's Word, which will help you apply it to your life and get the most out of it.
- Courage is not afraid to take a chance. A courageous, godly person will seek God, apply wisdom, and act boldly as the Holy Spirit leads.

Taking Courage in the Word

Read **Judges 20:22** (AMPC), and notice that the men "took courage and strengthened themselves." They did not wait for someone else to give them courage and strength. How can you take courage and strengthen yourself today?

_____

_____

_____

God wants to bring transformation to your life so you can live with purpose, joy, and strength. Based on **Romans 12:2**, what is the key to transformation?

_____

According to **Romans 5:8**, how do you know that, even though you are not perfect, God loves you?

_____

What has Jesus done for you, according to **2 Corinthians 5:21**?

_____

Chapter 12 teaches that focusing more on what you need to do than on what you want to avoid is important. Based on this understanding, why is the order of God's commands to Joshua important in **Joshua 1:9**? How can you follow this example as you fight fear?

_____

_____

_____

Read Esther 4:16–5:3. How did Esther develop greater courage and less fear? Why was this so important, and what was the result? How does she inspire you?

_____

_____

Fill in the blanks in **Deuteronomy 31:6**: "Be _____ and _____. Do not be _____ or _____ because of them, for the Lord your God goes with you; he will _____ leave you nor forsake you." Read the fourth paragraph of the section titled "Encouragement." What does this understanding of **Romans 8:15** (AMPC) mean to you, and how can it make a difference in your life?

_____

_____

What do these verses teach you about your relationship with God?
Ephesians 2:13

_____

Romans 8:15–17

_____

2 Corinthians 6:18

_____

Based on **Proverbs 18:21**, why is it important for you to speak encouraging words to others and to yourself?

_____

_____

What is the instruction in **1 Thessalonians 5:14**?

_____

_____

According to **Isaiah 35:3–4**, how are believers to treat those who are fearful?

_____

What does God say in **Joshua 1:8** that His people are to meditate on?

_____

This sentence appears in the section "Meditate and Declare": "**Mark 4:24** teaches us to be careful about what we hear and says that the measure of thought and study we give to the truth we hear is the measure of virtue and knowledge that will come back to us." How does this apply to meditating on God's Word?

_____

_____

Moving Forward in Freedom

How can you focus on building courage and gaining strength in your life instead of focusing on eliminating fear?

_____

_____

According to the fourth paragraph of chapter 12, "Fighting with fear will strengthen it instead of getting rid of it." What should you do instead?

_____

_____

At times when you feel courage and fear simultaneously, how can you strengthen your courage and weaken your fear?

_____

_____

_____

Fill in the blanks in this sentence from the last paragraph of the first section of chapter 12: "Courage _____ the _____ and _____ _____ beyond it."

Why is it so powerful for you to receive encouragement from people and so important for you to give encouragement to others?

_____

_____

How can you encourage people around you this week?

_____

_____

According to the section "Meditate and Declare," why is it important to meditate on God's Word?

_____

_____

Here is an example from chapter 12 of something you can meditate on and declare. It is composed of portions of several scriptures and is an effective way to meditate on them. If you declare this twice a day for thirty days, you will be amazed at what happens:

> I am a child of God, and He loves me. He is always with me, and therefore I will not fear. I can do all things through Christ, who is my strength. When I feel weak, He encourages me to keep pressing on. I am bold, courageous, and confident in Christ. No weapon formed against me shall prosper, because greater is He who is in me than he who is in the world.

What is one way you can be courageous and take a chance, yet still use wisdom in your life right now?

_____

_____

Have you ever overthought or overanalyzed something you needed to do to the point that you talked yourself out of doing it? How can you avoid that in the future?

_____

_____

In the third-to-last paragraph of chapter 12, what are the two ways God leads us? What does _discernment_ mean?

_____

_____

Keep This in Mind

Have I not commanded you? Be strong and courageous. Do not be afraid; do not be discouraged, for the Lord your God will be with you wherever you go.

Joshua 1:9

Courage is always available to you, and it is much stronger than fear. Focus more on building your courage than on eliminating fear.

CHAPTER 13

Learn to Be Secure and Confident

Setting Your Mind on Victory

Each time we face our fears, we gain strength, courage, and confidence in the doing.

Theodore Roosevelt

What does it mean, in practical ways, for you to face your fears?

_____

_____

How does facing your fears give you strength, courage, and confidence?

_____

_____

Doing It Afraid

Do you struggle with the fear Autumn describes—a fear of being open and vulnerable to others? Can you relate to feeling anxious about sharing matters of the heart? How does her story inspire you?

_____

_____

Revelation 12:11 gives Autumn courage. How can this verse give you courage, too?

_____

_____

Fear-Fighting Truths

These are the key truths from chapter 13. Check the ones you most need to believe and apply to your life.

- Feelings of insecurity and lack of confidence are symptoms of fear, and they are rooted in not feeling loved. They will keep you from accomplishing and enjoying all God has for you.
- The enemy tells you lies about who you are and what kinds of problems you have. If you believe those lies, they will become realities in your life. Knowing and believing the truth of God's Word will empower you to combat the lies of the enemy.
- If you grew up in an atmosphere of fear, you may struggle with various types of fear and may need to learn what kind of life God wants you to have. Study His Word so you will realize that He wants you to live with peace, joy, love, strength, and stability instead of fear.
- The key to overcoming insecurity and a lack of confidence is to place your faith and trust in God and in His love for you. Then, as the Holy Spirit guides you, begin to do things you have been afraid to do before.
- God will meet all of your needs, in His perfect timing, as you trust Him.
- When you take an action that is filled with faith, you gain more faith.
- Being a Christian does not mean you will never face difficulty, but it does mean you can always trust God to take care of you.

Taking Courage in the Word

What does **Psalm 40:1–2** reveal about God's heart toward you and the ways He wants to help you?

_____

_____

What do these verses teach you about how God wants you to live?
John 15:11

_____

John 16:24

_____

John 17:13

_____

Based on **Hebrews 13:5–6**, why should you not be afraid?

_____

According to **John 14:6**, who is Jesus to us?

_____

Based on **James 4:7**, what are the keys to getting the devil to flee from you?

_____

_____

The section "Use Your Faith" includes **Hebrews 11:1** (NKJV). Fill in the blanks:
Faith is "the _____ of things _____ for, the _____
_____ of things not _____."
According to **James 4:2**, what is the reason we do not always have certain things?

_____

Ephesians 3:20 says that God is able to do what?

_____

Read **Mark 11:24**. How does this verse encourage you? Remember that Scripture never says how much time will elapse between the time a person asks God for something in faith and the time they receive it, if it is His will, nor does it indicate *how* God will answer.

_____

_____

_____

Read **Ephesians 3:17–19**. As you read Paul's prayer for the Ephesians, what seems most important to him for them to know and experience?

_____

_____

How does **Psalm 4:8** comfort you?

_____

_____

What do these verses teach us we can depend on when we go through troubles?

Psalm 23:4

_____

Isaiah 41:10

_____

Based on **Psalm 37:1–3**, when we face difficulties, what are we to do?

_____

Read **Isaiah 43:1–2**. What can you count on God to do when you face difficulties?

_____

Moving Forward in Freedom

How does fear produce insecurity and low levels of confidence?

_____

_____

Why do insecurity and lack of confidence keep people from accomplishing much?

_____

_____

How does unconditional love help people overcome insecurity and lack of confidence?

_____

_____

What kinds of lies has the enemy convinced you are true about yourself? How are they adversely affecting your life?

_____

_____

Did you grow up in an atmosphere of fear? If so, what types of fear have you struggled with as a result of being raised in that environment?

_____

_____

According to the fifth paragraph of the section "Stop Listening to Lies," what are two keys to developing a loving and trusting relationship with God? How can you grow in your relationship with Him?

_____

_____

In what ways do you need to make an effort to overcome insecurity by doing something you haven't done before, trusting God as you do it?

_____

_____

_____

Never be afraid to ask God for what you want and need. He will answer you in His wisdom and according to His timing. What do you need to ask Him for right now?

_____

_____

How can you actively expect and be on the lookout for God's love to manifest in your life?

_____

_____

What are some situations in which you have trusted God in the past and seen Him move in powerful ways for you? How are you trusting Him right now?

_____

_____

How has God been with you through difficulties in the past, and how does this give you confidence that He will be with you through hard times you may face in the future?

_____

_____

Keep This in Mind

Do not fear, for I have redeemed you; I have summoned you by name; you are mine. When you pass through the waters, I will be with you; and when you pass through the rivers, they will not sweep over you. When you walk through the fire, you will not be burned.

Isaiah 43:1–2

Overcoming fear to the point that you feel secure and confident does not mean that you will never have troubles, but that God will bring you through them to a place of safety. God says that when you go through difficulties, He will be with you. The "going through" is not enjoyable, but the promise of coming out on the other side of a problem gives you hope, confidence, and security.

PART 3

Mindsets for Walking in Freedom from Fear

CHAPTER 14

You Can Love Fearlessly

Freedom from the Fear of Letting Yourself Love

Setting Your Mind on Victory

Love is the master key that opens the gates of happiness, of hatred, of jealousy, and, most easily of all, the gate of fear.

Oliver Wendell Holmes Sr.

When you think of fear as a gate—such as a gate that keeps you locked out of what you have been created to accomplish and enjoy—how can love unlock it?

_____

_____

How have you experienced love as a key to unlock something in your life?

_____

_____

Doing It Afraid

Joan reached a point where she unexpectedly became afraid of being alone at night, even though she had not previously dealt with that particular fear. Have you ever had a fear surprise you, meaning that you suddenly became afraid of something that had never frightened you before? What was it, and how did you deal with it?

_____

_____

Joan used an "old answer to an old lie" to fight her fear. Have you ever done that? What truth will replace the lie?

_____

_____

Fear-Fighting Truths

These are the key truths from chapter 14. Check the ones you most need to believe and apply to your life.

- People are often afraid to love others, because they are afraid they will be hurt, rejected, betrayed, abused, or abandoned. Love does require vulnerability and risk, but still is not something you should fear.
- The key to being able to love other people is to first receive God's love for yourself.
- Biologically speaking, you can live without love, but life would be lonely and miserable. Love gives your life meaning, purpose, fulfillment, and joy.
- Truly loving others requires letting go of selfish desires, attitudes, and habits.
- Everyone to whom you try to express love will not receive it, but keep trying to show love and kindness, even if people reject your generosity.
- When you love, you may be wounded. Jesus heals every hurt and wants you to forgive those who hurt you and offer them second chances, just as He forgives and offers them to you.

Taking Courage in the Word

Read **1 John 4:18** (AMPC). Why is there no fear in love? How have you experienced God's love overcoming fear in your life?

_____

Read **1 Corinthians 13:4–7.** What do these verses teach you about love?

Read **1 John 3:14.** Why would a life without love seem like death?

Fill in the blanks. According to **1 John 4:12,** "No one has ever seen God; but if we _____ one another, God _____ in us and his love is _____ in us."

Based on **1 John 4:19,** why do we love?

According to **1 John 3:23,** what does God expect of us?

How does **Galatians 5:16,** mentioned in the third paragraph of the section "Without Love There Is No Life," help you understand that what you focus on becomes what you will produce in your life?

According to **John 13:35,** how will the world know God?

How do these verses teach you to think about and treat others?
Philippians 2:3–4

Romans 12:3

It may be impossible to live and love without ever being wounded, but what does **Psalm 147:3** say God does for the brokenhearted?

According to **Romans 12:21,** how can you overcome evil?

Moving Forward in Freedom

Why does loving people require vulnerability?

_____

_____

According to the second paragraph of chapter 14, what is the key to learning to love and trust other people?

_____

What is the proper, loving response to people when they hurt us?

_____

_____

Why is isolation dangerous?

_____

_____

Dick Van Dyke says, "We all need something to do, someone to love, and something to hope for." What do you do that fills you with a sense of purpose? Who do you love? And what are you hoping for?

_____

_____

How can you focus more on loving God and receiving His love for you than on what you would like others (or God) to do for you?

_____

Are you a naturally giving person, or do you tend to be selfish? What are some ways you can change your thinking to be more concerned about others and their needs than about yourself and what you want?

_____

_____

How can you strike the appropriate balance between loving yourself in a healthy, biblical way and also caring for others and treating them as very important to God?

_____

_____

What are some practical ways you can help specific people in your life this week?

_____

_____

What random act of kindness can you do over the next several days?

_____

_____

Do you tend to erect invisible walls to keep people at a distance after they have hurt you? How can trusting God empower you to take down those walls and give people another chance?

_____

_____

The last paragraph of chapter 14 includes this statement: "Fearless love will defeat our enemy, Satan, who is hard at work spreading strife and hatred to levels most of us have never witnessed in our lifetime." Why is this true?

_____

_____

Keep This in Mind

Do not be overcome by evil, but overcome evil with good.

Romans 12:21

Remember, fearless love will defeat the enemy, Satan, who is hard at work spreading strife and hatred to levels most people have never witnessed. It's imperative to fight back, and the only force that overcomes evil is good. Walking in love is spiritual warfare, and it always triumphs over the enemy.

CHAPTER 15

You Can Live in Acceptance

Freedom from the Fear of Rejection

Setting Your Mind on Victory

Most fears of rejection rest on the desire for approval from other people. Don't base your self-esteem on their opinions.

Harvey Mackay

Would you agree that most fears of rejection come from wanting other people's approval?

_____

Have you ever based your self-esteem on someone else's opinion? If so, how did that affect you?

_____

_____

_____

Doing It Afraid

Davis' lifelong dream was to play football. Have you, like Davis, ever had to relinquish a dream for some reason? If so, what was your dream, and how did letting go of it force you to face fear?

_____

_____

How has a loss of some sort helped you in the past—or how can it help you now—discover your sense of security and purpose in Christ rather than what you do or what you're striving to accomplish?

_____

_____

Fear-Fighting Truths

These are the key truths from chapter 15. Check the ones you most need to believe and apply to your life.

- If you have experienced rejection and abandonment, please understand that this was never God's intention for you. He accepts you completely and loves you unconditionally, and He created you to live with the love and acceptance of others.
- The more you grow in confidence in God's love for you and begin to understand how He sees you, the less you will struggle with rejection from people around you.
- You are a unique and special person. When God created you, He created someone amazing!
- One of the best things you can do for your self-esteem is to think positive, Scripture-based thoughts about yourself *on purpose*.
- To walk by faith means to believe something before you see it. Choose today to believe all the good things God says about you, even if you do not yet see them manifesting in your life.

Taking Courage in the Word

How does **Isaiah 53:3** comfort and encourage you?

_____

_____

What does Jesus say in **John 6:37** about people who come to Him?

_____

_____

According to **John 19:26; 20:2; 21:7, 20**, the apostle John knew Jesus loved him. Why is it important to realize that Jesus loves you and to be secure in His love?

_____

_____

What can you believe and say about yourself, based on **Psalm 17:8**?

_____

_____

_____

What can you learn from these verses about how you are made? What are some of the very special, wonderful things about you?
Genesis 1:26–27, 31

_____

Psalm 139:13–14

_____

According to **Romans 12:3**, how should you think about yourself?

_____

The section "Positive Think Sessions" suggests finding Scripture-based confessions to speak aloud in addition to the five that are listed. What are some Bible verses you will adapt and confess for yourself?

_____

_____

Fill in the blanks: According to **2 Corinthians 5:7**, "We live by _____ _____, not by _____."

Fill in the blank: Based on **2 Corinthians 3:18**, you are being _____ _____ into Christ's image.

Romans 8:29 says you are predestined for what?

_____

Moving Forward in Freedom

Do you think you have ever lived with—or that you currently live with—a root of rejection? If so, how has it affected you?

_____

_____

The story about Lucille Ball demonstrates how insecurity can be a manifestation of a root of rejection. Insecurity is also a type of fear. How have you seen insecurity, rejection, and fear work together or feed off of each other in your life or in the life of someone close to you?

_____

_____

Have you ever felt that people would reject you if they knew "the real you"? If so, take a moment to write down some of the things you believe people would like about the real you instead of focusing on things you think they might reject.

_____

_____

Why is the idea that God loves us unconditionally difficult for people to accept? How can you help yourself grasp this life-changing truth?

_____

_____

Say to yourself today: "The Father of Jesus is very fond of me." Ask the Holy Spirit to make this truth revelation to you and to establish it deeply in your heart.

The enemy wants you to think you are an accident or a mistake. How does the truth about what God says about you refute the lies of the enemy, especially lies that you are an accident or a mistake?

_____

_____

_____

Think about some of the negative words that were spoken to you in your past, words that affected the way you thought about yourself. Now, speak the opposite, based on the truth of God's Word.

How can you strengthen your faith in what God says about you in His Word, making other people's opinions of you less and less important and making God's opinion about who you really are more important to you?

_____

_____

Keep This in Mind

For you created my inmost being; you knit me together in my mother's womb. I praise you because I am fearfully and wonderfully made; your works are wonderful, I know that full well.

Psalm 139:13–14

Because God loves you, there is no reason to fear rejection from other people. He created you, and He is on your side. It is time to see yourself as God sees you and let His opinion of you be more important than what anyone else thinks.

CHAPTER 16

You Can Be Yourself

Freedom from the Fear of What Other People Will Think, Say, or Do

Setting Your Mind on Victory

A man who is intimate with God will never be intimidated by men.

Leonard Ravenhill

Have you ever been intimidated by another person? How did it feel? How did it affect your behavior when you were around them?

_____

Why does intimacy with God help us stand strong against intimidation from other people?

_____

_____

Doing It Afraid

Have you, like Julie, ever known in your gut that something was not right, but moved forward anyway because of fear of what others would think? How did that turn out?

_____

When Julie realized she was not allowing God to bless her as He wanted to, she canceled her wedding, despite her fear of what people would say and money that would be lost. She ended up with a great blessing. How does her story give you courage?

_____

_____

Fear-Fighting Truths

These are the key truths from chapter 16. Check the ones you most need to believe and apply to your life.

- Wanting people to like you is a normal desire, but it can cause problems when you care so much about what they will think, say, or do that you allow their opinions to control you.
- God's plan for you is better than anything anyone else could ever think of—including you. If you try to please people instead of trying to please God, you may miss the wonderful destiny He has for your life.
- You can learn from the stories of many Bible characters that anyone is susceptible to the fear of what others will think, say, or do. You can also learn from them how to break free from that fear and move forward into all God has for you.
- Only you can decide who you will be. You can experience the joy of being yourself and celebrating the uniqueness God has given you, or you can develop the persona you think other people would like you to have.
- If you often feel intimidated by other people, the way to break free from it is to grow in intimacy with God.

Taking Courage in the Word

Read **Proverbs 29:25**. How have you observed the fear of man (meaning the fear of what other people will think, say, or do) to be a snare in your life? How has trusting the Lord kept you safe?

_____

_____

Based on what Paul writes in **Galatians 1:10**, what could have kept him from becoming an apostle and having a ministry that gave him great joy and provided the church with great blessings and strength?

_____

_____

Read **Exodus 4:10–16**. What was Moses afraid of, and how did God intervene to make sure Moses' fear did not stop His plan for His people?

_____

_____

What does the story in **Luke 22:54–62** reveal about the apostle Peter's fears? How do you relate to his struggles and the way he felt about allowing fear to control him?

_____

_____

According to **Colossians 3:23–24**, when you choose to work for the Lord and not for other people, where will your reward come from?

_____

How does **1 Corinthians 10:24** say a Christian should live in relationship to others? What are some practical ways you can do this for someone else soon?

_____

_____

What can we learn from **Proverbs 18:24** (NASB) about the difference between our relationships with our natural friends and our relationship with Jesus as our heavenly friend?

_____

_____

What does **Psalm 27:4** reveal about David's relationship with God and the only thing he wanted in his life?

_____

Read **Matthew 6:33**. Are you seeking God and His kingdom above everything else in your life? If not, how might you make this more of a priority?

_____

_____

Moving Forward in Freedom

On a scale of 1–10, with 1 being "not at all" and 10 being "very much," how much do you allow the opinions of other people to control you?

_____

What experiences in your upbringing have affected the way you view what other people think or say about you, or what they do to you?

_____

_____

Failing to confront the controlling people who intimidate you through fear of what they may think, say, or do can make you miserable. What one step can you take this week to confront the ways someone is trying to control you?

_____

_____

When people come against you as you seek to do God's will, it's usually not human beings that oppose you. Who is it?

_____

Have you ever lost friends because you chose to follow God instead of allowing those friends to control you? What were the circumstances, and how was God faithful to you in the midst of those situations?

_____

_____

You can choose to be the person God created you to be or try to be someone you think other people want you to be. Which will you choose and why?

_____

_____

Are you doing anything for another person or a group of people that you do not have peace about? Why are you doing it, and what needs to change?

_____

_____

Why is intimacy with God a safeguard against those who try to intimidate you?

_____

_____

What changes can you make in your life in order to spend more time in God's presence and to develop greater intimacy with Him?

_____

_____

Keep This in Mind

Fear of man will prove to be a snare, but whoever trusts in the Lord is kept safe.

Proverbs 29:25

If you are tired of trying to please the people around you in unhealthy ways, let this chapter be a turning point for you. One word from God can change your life, and He may be speaking to you through the words of this study. His grace is available to help you let go of the fear of what other people will think, say, or do and go deeper in your friendship with God.

CHAPTER 17

You Can Trade Fear for Fear

Freedom from the Wrong Kinds of Fear

Setting Your Mind on Victory

Men are swayed more by fear than by reverence.

Aristotle

What is the difference between the reverential fear of God and the wrong kinds of fear?

_____

_____

_____

Why do you think more people are swayed by the wrong kinds of fear than by the fear of the Lord?

_____

_____

Doing It Afraid

Have you, like Beth, ever found yourself afraid of God in the wrong kind of way? What were the circumstances and how did that unhealthy fear affect you?

_____

_____

How has God shown Himself to be awesome in your life? What causes you to say, "God, You're awesome"?

_____

_____

_____

_____

Fear-Fighting Truths

These are the key truths from chapter 17. Check the ones you most need to believe and apply to your life.

- Of all the various types of fear that exist, there is only one that is good and right, and it is more valuable to us than we may realize: the reverential fear of the Lord.
- The reverential fear of God will set you free from wrong and tormenting kinds of fear.
- The word *fear* means something different in the context of reverence than in everyday, modern uses of the word. It is not fright as we understand it today; it is a deeply respectful and awe-inspiring attitude toward God.
- People who have casual or disrespectful attitudes toward certain aspects of life may also have casual or irreverent attitudes toward God and His presence.
- People who do not respect God are not likely to respect other people, either.
- Power and effectiveness in ministry are directly related to our reverential fear of God.
- Growing in the reverential fear of the Lord breaks the torment of the wrong kinds of fear.

Taking Courage in the Word

Read **Proverbs 9:10**. Why is the reverential fear of the Lord referred to as "the beginning of wisdom"? Do you think it is possible for a person to be truly wise without a proper fear of the Lord?

_____

_____

_____

Using a concordance or an Internet search, find and list five scriptures about the reverential fear of God.

_____

_____

How does **Luke 18:2** support the idea that if we don't fear God, we won't respect people, either?

_____

_____

According to **Acts 9:31**, what was a major key to the growth of the early church?

_____

How did Abraham demonstrate his reverential fear of the Lord in the story presented in **Genesis 22:1–12**?

_____

_____

In **1 Peter 2:17**, what simple formula for living does the apostle Peter offer?

_____

How did the reverential fear of God affect the apostle John in **Revelation 1:17–18**?

_____

In **Psalm 138:2**, how does the psalmist physically express his reverence for God?

_____

Read **Hebrews 10:30–31** (ESV). According to the last two paragraphs of chapter 17, why is it a "fearful thing" to fall into God's hands?

_____

_____

Moving Forward in Freedom

According to the first sentence of chapter 17, what is the most important thing there is?

_____

_____

_____

Fill in the blanks based on the first paragraph of chapter 17: When we exchange the fear of the Lord for other types of fear, we are trading the _____ _____ kind of fear for the _____ kind of fear.

What is the difference between the reverential fear of God and the wrong kinds of fear?

_____

_____

Fill in the blanks in Joy Dawson's definition of the fear of the Lord from her book *Forever Ruined for the Ordinary*: "The fear of the Lord means being more _____ with _____ reactions to our actions than with _____ _____ reactions."

How will the reverential fear of God affect the way we treat other people, whom He loves?

_____

_____

How should the fear of the Lord affect our behavior in church and/or in ministry?

_____

_____

Fill in the blanks from the last paragraph of the section "Reverential Fear and Power": "If you feel the need for more power in your life or ministry, make sure you have a proper _____ _____ _____ _____ of _____."

According to the section "Two Kinds of Fear," what is the difference between the servile fear of God and the filial fear of God?

_____

_____

Keep This in Mind

The fear of the Lord is the beginning of wisdom, and knowledge of the Holy One is understanding.

Proverbs 9:10

The only right kind of fear to have is the reverential fear of the Lord, which causes us to honor Him and stand in awe of Him. This type of fear empowers us to overcome all wrong types of fear.

CHAPTER 18

You Can Stop Worrying about Money

Freedom from Financial Fears

Setting Your Mind on Victory

Wealth consists not in having great possessions, but in having few wants.

Epictetus

Have you ever stopped to think what the words *wealth* and *rich* mean to you? When you hear these words, do you think about possessions or money, or do you think about having few wants?

_____

_____

How does the quotation by Epictetus define for you in practical terms what true wealth is?

_____

_____

Doing It Afraid

Have you ever felt bombarded with fear-filled what-if questions, as Chuck did? How did you process them and move beyond them?

_____

_____

Chuck had to learn to ignore popular opinion and do what was right for his family. What can you learn from his story about doing what is right for you, even if people around you don't agree or understand?

_____

_____

How does the fact that Chuck's nine years as a stay-at-home dad were "nine of the best years" of his life inspire you to do something afraid?

_____

_____

Fear-Fighting Truths

These are the key truths from chapter 18. Check the ones you most need to believe and apply to your life.

- God's Word contains many scriptures on the stewardship of financial resources, handling money wisely, and the blessings and responsibilities of being generous to others. Obviously, the way you handle finances is important to Him, and He wants to bless you.
- Develop the habit of praying about your finances frequently, not just when you have a financial need. Ask God to bless your investments, to protect your savings, to help you find good deals, and to bless your work as it produces income.
- People often say they would manage their money better if they had more to manage. This isn't true. God is looking for people who will be faithful when they have little before He blesses them with increase.
- It is important to enjoy the fruit of your labors and the money you make. Don't spend more than you have or spend something God is leading you to save, give to His work, or use to bless someone else, but don't live a life of total denial, either.

- Trust God in every circumstance and at all times to meet your needs, and resist the temptation to be afraid of financial loss or lack.
- It is a good idea to pray that God will give you everything you need, while also asking Him not to give you more than you can handle and still keep Him first.
- Debt is difficult to deal with. It will keep you enslaved to your creditors. It will take diligence to get out of debt, but God will help you if you ask Him to do so. Keep working on it until you become financially free!

Taking Courage in the Word

List several needs you currently have. Do you believe God will meet them and that, in Christ, you have everything you need?

_____

_____

Read **2 Corinthians 9:6–11**. What does this passage teach about the connection between generosity and blessing? Who is responsible to sow seeds of generosity, and who is the one who brings blessing and increase? Even if you have to do it afraid, how can you give from a generous heart today?

_____

_____

_____

Using wisdom is important in financial matters, but people often make mistakes. If you have made financial decisions you regret and have now asked God to help you in this area, how does **Romans 8:28** encourage you?

_____

_____

What can you learn about praying for provision for yourself from **Matthew 6:9–13**?

_____

_____

What practical steps can you take in your everyday life to seek God's King-dom? As you seek His Kingdom first, what can you count on as a result, based on **Matthew 6:33**?

_____

There may be things you want in life, but what should your first priority be, according to **Psalm 37:4**?

_____

What does **Luke 16:10** say about the best way to manage your resources, finances, and possessions?

_____

How does **Hebrews 13:5** (AMPC) encourage you not to worry about finances and strengthen your faith?

_____

_____

How does **Psalm 23:1** (NKJV) help you fight the fear of lack?

_____

_____

_____

According to **2 Corinthians 5:15**, what is one reason Jesus died for you?

_____

Based on **Romans 13:8**, what is the only thing the Bible encourages people to owe?

_____

What does **Proverbs 22:7** say about being in debt?

_____

Moving Forward in Freedom

On a scale of 1–10, with 1 being "not at all" and 10 being "very much," how worried are you about your financial situation?

_____

What are some specific ways you could apply greater wisdom in handling the financial resources you currently have?

_____

_____

How can you begin to pray more often or more specifically about your financial situation?

_____

_____

Did you grow up in an atmosphere of lack, one of sufficiency, or one of plenty? How did the resources—or lack of resources—available to you as a young person affect the way you view and handle finances today? What positive or negative lessons did you learn from the way your parents related to money?

_____

_____

In terms of saving and spending, where are you on a scale of 1–10, with 1 being a person who saves as much as possible and 10 being a person who does not save at all?

_____

How can you apply Dave's formula for finances, mentioned in the second-to-last paragraph of the section "My Fears Concerning Money," to your life: "Save some, spend some, and give some within your borders"?

_____

_____

Biblical wisdom instructs us to give as the Holy Spirit leads us, and to pray instead of worry. What can you do in your everyday life to apply this lesson about being free from fear of lack?

_____

_____

Explain how you have found Corrie ten Boom's words to be true: "Worry does not empty tomorrow of its sorrow. It empties today of its strength."

_____

_____

People may lack money, but they may also lack other resources as well. What do you feel you lack, if anything? How can you demonstrate your trust in God to meet your needs?

_____

_____

What can you learn about the meaning of the Old Testament name for God, El Shaddai, from the section "An Abundant God"?

_____

_____

The section "An Abundant God" includes teaching on "the land of even." What is that and what do you need to do when you are in that place?

_____

_____

In your own words, write a sentence or two to describe how you would act if you were as generous as you could possibly be. If you cannot immediately act on everything you write, what parts of it can you act on right away?

_____

_____

If your finances are tight, what other resources do you have through which you can be generous to others?

_____

_____

List a few people you would like to bless this week. What practical steps can you take to support, encourage, or help them?

_____

_____

Why is being in debt such a negative experience?

_____

_____

If you are in debt, what steps can you take to gradually pay off what you owe and move into a position of being able to save, invest, and give generously?

_____

_____

Keep This in Mind

And my God will meet all your needs according to the riches of his glory in Christ Jesus.

Philippians 4:19

Don't be afraid to ask God for what you want or need, but don't forget to be very thankful for what you have and to give generously to others, trusting God to provide for you and meet your every need.

CHAPTER 19

You Can Believe Good Things Are Ahead

Freedom from Fear of the Future

Setting Your Mind on Victory

May your choices reflect your hopes, not your fears.

Nelson Mandela

Why is it important for your choice to reflect your hopes instead of your fears?

_____

_____

_____

What deliberate choices can you make this week that will represent what you hope for, not what you fear?

_____

_____

_____

Doing It Afraid

Can you relate to what happened to Matt when he decided to follow God *on the inside* and fear began to cave in on him *on the outside*? If so, describe that experience in your life.

_____

_____

Have you ever leaned into fear instead of leaning into God? How can you choose this week to lean into Him instead of allowing fear to consume you?

_____

_____

For Matt, fear manifested in the form of questions. What questions is fear asking you right now?

_____

_____

At a Joyce Meyer conference, Matt heard: "Your feelings change, but God's promise will always sustain you." How has this proven true in your experience?

_____

_____

Fear-Fighting Truths

These are the key truths from chapter 19. Check the ones you most need to believe and apply to your life.

- You may be uncertain about many things, but you can be sure of this: God has a plan for your life. You can trust that it is a good plan and that your future is filled with hope.
- Learning to trust God helps us build a solid relationship of reliance on Him even through the most trying times and enables us to stay at peace in fearful circumstances.
- Learning to trust God is not easy, but it is the doorway to the good life He has for you.
- God wants you to trust Him for everything. This doesn't relieve you of responsibilities in your life; it simply means you trust Him more than you trust yourself or anyone or anything else.
- Trusting God is a privilege.

- No matter where life takes you, God will go before you.
- People who do not walk with God can rely only on their fears, thoughts, plans, and reasoning when thinking about the future. As a believer, you have another option—trusting God.
- The future is full of uncertainty, and there will be many things in life that you will not know. But you can know God, you can know His Word, and you can follow His Spirit. This will empower you to trust Him with everything you do not know.

Taking Courage in the Word

One of the best Bible verses you can memorize is **Jeremiah 29:11**. Write it on the lines below and take time to memorize it this week.

_____

_____

_____

According to **Deuteronomy 31:8**, why is there no reason ever to be afraid or discouraged?

_____

_____

_____

What do these verses teach about consulting mediums, spiritists, or other ungodly sources to find out about your future? Why is doing this spiritually dangerous?

Leviticus 19:31

_____

Deuteronomy 18:10–14

_____

There are many things we want to know, but cannot. According to **1 Corinthians 2:2**, what is the most important thing we can know?

_____

Moving Forward in Freedom

According to the first paragraph of chapter 19, God's plan for you is for
_____, and He has in store for you a future filled with _____.
What is the oldest and strongest fear? Do you ever struggle with it, and if so,
how would you describe that struggle?

_____

_____

What are two words, in addition to *trust*, mentioned in the first section of
chapter 19, that the Bible uses to communicate the idea of trusting God?

_____

What are some of the benefits of trusting God?

_____

_____

If your boss asked to see you at four o'clock on a Friday afternoon, what
would be your first thought about that meeting? What is the most positive
thought you could have about that situation, and how would that positive
mindset help you?

_____

_____

_____

Human nature causes us to think negatively instead of positively in many
circumstances. Can you relate to this? How can you deliberately choose to
think something good instead of something bad in a situation you are facing?

_____

_____

_____

As a Christian, how can you think differently about the future than a person
who has not yet chosen to walk with God can?

_____

_____

What can you learn from this statement in the fourth paragraph of the section "Get Comfortable Not Knowing": "We don't need to know the future as long as we know the One who does know it"?

_____

_____

Keep This in Mind

"For I know the plans I have for you," declares the Lord, "plans to prosper you and not to harm you, plans to give you hope and a future."

Jeremiah 29:11

If you are like most people, you would like to know what the future has in store for you. You may have a sense about what your career will be or the kinds of relationships you will have with others, but concerning the future, God leaves out most details and simply says that His plan is for good and not for evil. You can count on the truth that He has in store for you a future filled with hope!

CHAPTER 20

You Can Trust God in Every Situation

Freedom from the Fear that Bad Things Will Happen

Setting Your Mind on Victory

But now having seen him which is invisible I fear not what man can do unto me.

Anne Hutchinson

Anne Hutchinson suffered greatly and faced many troubles during her lifetime. She continually trusted in God and refused to fear what people might do to her. Why was she not afraid?

_____

_____

How does knowing God strengthen you against the fear that something bad might happen to you?

_____

_____

Doing It Afraid

How does Rebecca's story inspire you to take a risk and step out in faith, trusting God when you have no idea what's ahead for you?

_____

_____

Hearing the encouragement to "do it afraid" caused Rebecca to feel "empowered with a new mindset." How does the concept of doing something afraid empower you with new thoughts?

_____

_____

Rebecca writes, "I found that the bigger I let God be in my life, the smaller my fear became, until it was gone." How can you allow God to become bigger in your life this week?

_____

_____

Fear-Fighting Truths

These are the key truths from chapter 20. Check the ones you most need to believe and apply to your life.

- In this world, there is no way to avoid trouble, but Jesus gives you His peace and His presence to be with you through it all.
- Jesus has warned us ahead of time that we will encounter trouble. This means you do not need to be afraid. You can be prepared to face it.
- When you are trapped in fear, you will see no way out of trouble, but when you live by faith, you are confident that God will make a way for you.
- When life is problem-free, the idea of trusting God seems easy. But when you face difficulties and your faith is challenged, trusting Him must be a deliberate decision, and you may have to make it several times a day.
- The best way to face difficulty is to decide ahead of time what you will do. You can set your mind before trouble comes that you will stand strong in Christ and face any challenge with faith, never giving up.
- God can take even the most painful aspects of your life and use them in wonderful ways.

- Trouble and problems are temporary. When God brings you through them to the other side, you will likely be stronger and wiser than you would have been had you not faced them, and you will be better prepared for the good things He has in store for you in the future.

Taking Courage in the Word

Read **Psalm 50:15**. Think about how hopeless you would feel if you could not cry out to God in times of trouble. Why is being able to call on Him during difficult times so important and so powerful?

_____

_____

_____

In **John 16:33**, what does Jesus say about trouble and the proper way to respond to it? Why should a believer respond this way?

_____

_____

_____

What instruction does Jesus offer in **John 14:27**?

_____

Which of the things Paul mentions in **2 Timothy 3:2–4** do you see happening in the world today?

_____

What does **1 Corinthians 10:13** tell you that you can count on?

_____

What does David declare in **Psalm 23:4**? Will you agree with him?

_____

We know that God is the source of all wisdom. What promise does **Proverbs 1:33** (AMPC) make to those who pay attention to wisdom?

_____

_____

What can you learn about God's protection from these verses?
Genesis 19:12–16

_____

Genesis 7:1–5

_____

Exodus 8, 9

_____

According to **James 1:2–3**, why should you have a positive attitude toward trouble?

_____

_____

What can you learn about giving and receiving comfort from **2 Corinthians 1:3–4**?

_____

_____

_____

What do these passages teach about the testing of a believer's faith?
1 Peter 4:12

_____

1 Peter 1:6–7

_____

Declaring the words of **Philippians 4:13** (AMPC) will help you develop a mindset of perseverance and victory before trouble comes. Write the verse on the lines below and commit it to memory during the next few weeks.

_____

_____

_____

According to **Romans 8:28, 37**, what gives us hope if we do face things that are evil or that we do not understand?

_____

Why does **Genesis 50:20** give you hope?

_____

_____

According to **Philippians 1:28** (AMPC), how should you respond to the ene-my's schemes, and what does that response communicate to him?

_____

_____

Moving Forward in Freedom

How does God's peace differ from the so-called peace the world offers?

_____

_____

Why does Jesus warn us of trouble ahead of time?

_____

_____

Why do people who trust in Jesus have no need to fear problems and difficulties?

_____

_____

What are some wise ways for Christians to respond to the troubles currently in the world?

_____

_____

What does this statement mean, and how can you apply it to your life: "Fear is a dead end, but faith always has a future"?

_____

_____

_____

In the section titled "I Will Fear No Evil," what is God's definition of evil?

_____

_____

Think about a time when you had to trust God when you were struggling, your faith was being tested, and trusting God was difficult. What did you learn from that experience?

_____

_____

What is the upside of going through trials?

_____

_____

_____

What can you determine today about how you will face trouble that may come in the future?

_____

_____

_____

What are some positive ways God has used trials in your life?

_____

_____

_____

Why is the fear of a potential problem often worse than the problem itself?

_____

_____

"Our addiction to comfort often keeps us from the freedom and break-throughs that we need." How have you seen this statement from the last paragraph of chapter 20 to be true in your life or in the life of someone you know?

_____

_____

_____

To become everything you want to be or to have everything you want, you may have to endure some uncomfortable circumstances or some unpleasant discipline. What do you want to become or to have, and what will you need to go through in order to have the blessings it will ultimately bring to your life?

_____

_____

Keep This in Mind

But as for you, you meant evil against me; but God meant it for good, in order to bring it about as it is this day, to save many people alive.

Genesis 50:20 (NKJV)

As a believer, you are anointed with God's power. This means you can face whatever you need to face in life, even the troubles that will inevitably come, and face them with a good attitude, fearing nothing and trusting that God is always with you, working for your good.

CHAPTER 21

You Can Relax

Freedom from the Fear of Not Doing Enough

Setting Your Mind on Victory

First of all, let me assert my firm belief that the only thing we have to fear is fear itself—nameless, unreasoning, unjustified terror which paralyzes needed efforts to convert retreat into advance.

Franklin D. Roosevelt

What does it mean that "the only thing we have to fear is fear itself"? Have you found this to be true in your life?

_____

_____

In what ways have you realized that fear is nameless, unreasoning, or unjustified?

_____

_____

_____

Doing It Afraid

Are you a planner, like Mike, and does that cause you to worry about all the things that could happen?

_____

Mike says that he truly does trust God, but sometimes his actions indicate otherwise. How can you relate to this?

_____

_____

How can you find the balance between trusting God with all your heart and wisely preparing for situations that may arise?

_____

_____

Fear-Fighting Truths

These are the key truths from chapter 21. Check the ones you most need to believe and apply to your life.

- Many people, maybe even you, struggle with wondering whether they are doing enough. This is often rooted in the fear that God will not be pleased with them if they are not doing enough.
- The world wants you to believe that your value is tied to how much you work or how much you produce. That's why many people feel guilty about resting or are hesitant to enjoy their lives. This is not a healthy, biblical viewpoint.
- No matter what the enemy has stolen from you, God wants to redeem it.
- There is no way to measure what is "enough." What's important is to do the best you can do each day, while also giving yourself time to rest and enjoy your life.
- Many people worry that they are not doing enough for God to accept them. The good news is that through faith in Jesus, you are made completely acceptable to Him. Your acceptance is based on your relationship with Him, not through anything you do or don't do.
- When you are tired and weary, Jesus does not want you to find something else to do so you can feel you've done enough. He wants you to

come to Him and receive the rest He offers, which is complete rest and refreshment for every aspect of your life.

- Every requirement God has ever placed on you has already been met through Jesus Christ.
- The only work anyone can do that is truly acceptable to God is work done from a pure heart.
- The world and the enemy can be very hard on you. There's no need to make things worse by being hard on yourself. Do your best each day, and be kind and merciful toward yourself, as God is merciful to you.

Taking Courage in the Word

Why did Christ set us free, according to **Galatians 5:1**, and what are we to do with the freedom He gives us? How can you stand firm in freedom?

_____

_____

_____

John 14:13–14 (AMPC) is a passage about praying in Jesus' name. Based on the fourth paragraph of the section "Made Acceptable," what does it mean to pray in His name?

_____

Fill in the blank: According to **Matthew 11:28–29** (NIV), Jesus wants you to come to Him when you feel _____ and _____. What will you find when you come to Him?

_____

_____

What can you learn from **1 Corinthians 3:12–15** about the work you do?

_____

Based on the second-to-last paragraph in the section "Work Done from a Pure Heart," why would you be wise to follow David's example in **Psalm 139:23–24?**

How does **Colossians 2:13–14** assure you that God loves you unconditionally and accepts you completely?

What do you learn from **Hebrews 4:15** about the difference between the temptations Jesus dealt with and the weaknesses we face?

According to **2 Corinthians 3:18**, what is happening to you as you follow Jesus?

What is God's promise in **1 John 4:18**?

What did God speak to His Son in **Matthew 3:17**? What kind of example did Jesus set for all believers when He chose to receive those words and not resist them?

Moving Forward in Freedom

Do you ever wonder whether you are doing enough? How do you measure or evaluate that?

Do you work too much, feel guilty about resting, or struggle to allow yourself to enjoy your life? If so, why do you think this is?

Our culture may try to convince us that the more we work, the more valuable we are. How can you counteract that message and develop a healthier, more biblical perspective?

_____

_____

_____

What has the enemy stolen from you? How can you pray and believe that God will redeem what has been taken?

_____

_____

_____

No matter how much we do, it may never seem like enough. What can you do to make sure you get the rest, refreshment, and enjoyment of life that you need without feeling guilty or thinking you don't deserve it?

_____

_____

_____

When the enemy tries to tell you that you're not doing enough or not being good enough for God to accept you, how do you know he is lying?

_____

_____

_____

How can we be sure we are working from a pure heart?

_____

_____

Why is fear "Satan's tool of torment," as mentioned in the section "Don't Be So Hard on Yourself"?

_____

The Bible promises that God is pleased with us. Why?

_____

_____

Keep This in Mind

For it is by grace you have been saved, through faith—and this is not from yourselves, it is the gift of God—not by works, so that no one can boast.

Ephesians 2:8–9

You will find great comfort and confidence in God's love as you choose to believe and say to yourself, quietly in your heart, "God is pleased with me." There is nothing you can do to make Him any more or less pleased than He already is. It is a gift of grace, which you receive by faith. You can even go a step further and speak this confession into the atmosphere when you are alone. That will help set you free from the fear that you are not doing enough.

CHAPTER 22

You Can Build Healthy Relationships

Freedom from the Fear of Trusting God and Others

Setting Your Mind on Victory

Have enough courage to trust love one more time, and always one more time.

Maya Angelou

Have you ever had to make a decision about whether or not to trust love one more time? What was that like, and what was the result?

_____

_____

What could be the outcome of not choosing to trust love one more time?

_____

_____

What could happen if you did decide to risk trusting love one more time? Is the potential reward greater than the risk?

_____

_____

Doing It Afraid

Ashley recognized that her fear of intimacy had its root in a family crisis that developed during her teenage years. What situation in your past may still be negatively impacting the way you view your relationships today and how you behave in them?

_____

_____

_____

Have you ever been so hurt or disappointed in a relationship that you were reluctant to commit to other relationships or afraid to love again? How can you allow God to give you the courage to trust Him again and to trust once more?

_____

_____

_____

Fear-Fighting Truths

These are the key truths from chapter 22. Check the ones you most need to believe and apply to your life.

- If you have difficulty connecting with God or with others in healthy, intimate relationships or staying committed to loved ones, God is able to heal the pain of past relationships and restore your ability to trust.
- You can open your heart to God and have a deep, personal relationship with Him without fear that He will ever betray you, hurt you, or abandon you.
- You can trust God to handle any vindication that may be needed in your life and to bring justice wherever He sees that justice is needed.
- The only way to trust God is to try it. He will prove Himself trustworthy to you.
- Many people think, *If I trust someone, I will get hurt.* It's possible that you will get hurt, but God can heal you if you do. It's also likely that refusing to trust people will cause you to miss some of the great blessings that come from friendship and other types of relationships.

- When you handle situations God's way instead of the world's way or the way your natural mind may think is right, you will end up with God's best.
- You can safely trust in God all the time, in every situation. Many people can be trusted, too, but trust in others should build gradually and wisely. Always trust God more than you trust another human being.

Taking Courage in the Word

Read **Isaiah 26:3**. Why does trusting in God keep our minds steadfast and in perfect peace? What happens to our minds and to our peace when we do not trust in God?

_____

_____

_____

According to **1 Peter 5:7**, what should we do when we feel burdened with cares?

_____

What is God's promise in **James 4:8**?

_____

What does Jesus say in **John 10:3–4** about people who belong to Him?

_____

Based on **Philippians 3:10** (AMPC), what was the apostle Paul's "determined purpose"? How can you commit to that same purpose?

_____

_____

How does **1 Peter 2:23** say that Jesus responded when He was mistreated and falsely accused?

_____

According to **Isaiah 61:8**, how does God feel about justice and how does that cause Him to act?

What does **1 Peter 5:6** say God will do if we humble ourselves before Him?

How does **Luke 22:26** characterize a truly great person?

Based on **2 Timothy 4:14–17**, what was Paul's attitude toward Alexander the metalworker, after he treated him badly?

Why didn't Jesus entrust Himself fully to His disciples, according to **John 2:24** (AMPC)? How can you follow this example?

Moving Forward in Freedom

Why is life difficult for people who cannot trust God and/or others?

What are some causes of the inability to trust or of the fear of trusting?

Fill in the blanks in this sentence from the first section of chapter 22: "We need to develop an _____, _____ relationship with _____ before we can do the same with people."

What are some reasons people are reluctant to develop close relationships with others?

Does the idea of intimate relationships with other people make you nervous? Or do you work hard to keep people at a distance that feels safe to you? If so, why?

_____

_____

_____

According to the first paragraph of the section "Intimacy with God," why did Jesus die?

_____

What is one way you can develop more intimacy with God this week?

_____

_____

Fill in the blanks in this sentence from the section "Intimacy with God": "An _____, _____ relationship with God is what sets us free from many _____ fears and _____ _____."

Consider this sentence from the section "Intimacy with God" in chapter 22: "Think about how free you would feel if you never felt compelled to make sure they did not hurt you again because you trust God to bring justice in His perfect timing." When you think about that, how free would you feel, and how would that kind of freedom help you enjoy your life?

_____

_____

In what situation in your life do you need to trust God to bring vindication and/or justice?

_____

_____

Describe a situation in which you trusted God and realized that He did not fail.

_____

_____

Have you ever decided you would not trust people again because someone hurt you in the past? How did that decision affect your life?

_____

_____

Why is it important to extend mercy and forgiveness to the people who hurt you?

_____

_____

According to the first paragraph of the section "Trusting People," what is one reason we should use caution when it comes to trusting people completely?

_____

_____

How do close, intimate connections with people you trust make your life better?

_____

_____

Keep This in Mind

Come near to God and he will come near to you.

James 4:8

Resist the temptation to isolate yourself for fear of being hurt or taken advantage of. Develop an intimate relationship with God and close relationships with other people, and if you need to, "do it afraid." If one relationship doesn't work out, don't assume others will be the same way. God has people especially set aside to be your good friends, so pray and ask for His guidance. Don't let fear make you afraid to trust!

CHAPTER 23

You Can Rest in the Promise of Eternity

Freedom from the Fear of Death

Setting Your Mind on Victory

Do not be afraid to give up the good to go for the great.

John D. Rockefeller

Have you ever settled for something good when you could have had something great? What happened, and how do you feel about it now?

_____

_____

Life on earth may seem good to you, but heaven will be even greater. How can you begin now to set your mind on heaven and on things above instead of allowing it to be weighed down with excessive earthly concerns?

_____

_____

Doing It Afraid

Looking at the Slingshot and realizing that Shiloh was wrestling with fear, his father said, "It's your choice, but make sure you don't have regrets later from missing out on something fun." The same principle could apply to everyone who wrestles with the fear of death. Being afraid of death will rob you of the joy of living. How does the fear of death keep people from enjoying life?

If you struggle with the fear of death, what steps could you take this week to overcome fear and deliberately enjoy your life?

Shiloh also writes, "I trusted my dad when I was afraid, and he did not let me down." How have you trusted God, your heavenly Father, when you were afraid and found that He has never let you down?

Fear-Fighting Truths

These are the key truths from chapter 23. Check the ones you most need to believe and apply to your life.

- Your life on earth is temporary, and death comes to everyone. If you are a Christian, there is no need to fear death because you have the hope and promise of spending eternity with God in heaven after your earthly body ceases to exist.
- The apostle Paul offers a great example for any believer to follow: He looked forward to the joys of heaven, but he also wanted to stay on earth as long as God wanted him to so he could continue to help others. As long as you are alive on this earth, you can serve God and help people. When God calls you to your eternal home at the end of your earthly life, you will experience the joys of heaven.
- Hell is a real place. Contrary to what some people believe, God does not send anyone to hell. It is simply an eternal destination for people who choose not to follow Jesus as their Lord and Savior. As a believer, you can pray for those who do not know Him—that they will receive His gift of salvation and eternal life in His presence.

- Jesus died a human death, just as you and I will someday. But Jesus did not remain dead. Three days after His crucifixion, He defeated death and was resurrected! His resurrection means you never need to fear death; it has no power over you and is just the beginning of your eternal life.

- Many people—perhaps you—are more afraid of dying than of death. As a believer, you can take comfort in the fact that God will not only be with you throughout your life, but He will also be with you in that final moment and usher you into His glorious presence, where you will live forever.

Taking Courage in the Word

Read **Hebrews 2:15** (AMPC). Have you ever known anyone held in bondage by the fear of death? Why would that be such a tragic way to live?

_____

_____

According to **Revelation 21:4**, what will heaven be like?

_____

What does **Ecclesiastes 3:11** mean when it says God has "set eternity in the human heart"?

_____

_____

Read **Philippians 1:21–24**. What does the apostle Paul's perspective on life and death teach you, and how does it encourage and comfort you?

_____

_____

What do these scriptures teach about sin and Jesus' sacrifice for the sin of humanity?
Isaiah 53:5–12

_____

Ephesians 5:2

_____

1 John 4:10

_____

What can you learn about God's heart and desire for all people from 2 Peter 3:9?

_____

_____

How do these verses describe hell?
Luke 13:28

_____

Matthew 25:41

_____

Mark 9:43

_____

Jude 7

_____

Luke 16:19–31

_____

Luke 16:24 (AMPC)

_____

How does **Revelation 20:15** describe the destiny of unrepentant sinners?

_____

According to **John 20:6–7**, what did Jesus leave behind in the empty tomb? Why is this significant?

_____

_____

Describe how **John 14:1–3** gives you hope and peace.

_____

_____

_____

Moving Forward in Freedom

How does *Vine's Complete Expository Dictionary* define the word *death*?

_____

According to God's promises, what happens to a believer after his or her earthly life ceases to exist?

_____

_____

How does the fact that Jesus had an earthly body and died a physical death help you fight the fear of death?

_____

_____

According to the first section of chapter 23, why do people never feel 100 percent satisfied with their lives on earth?

_____

_____

Death is unavoidable. It will happen, so what is the best attitude to have about it?

_____

_____

What can you learn from the way the apostle Paul thought about life and death in the section "The Apostle Paul Talked about Death"?

_____

_____

Why do believers in Jesus need to be aware that hell exists, but not need to be personally concerned about it or afraid of it?

_____

_____

_____

List several nonbelievers you will pray for, believing for their salvation and eternal life in heaven.

_____

_____

Why are you thankful that Jesus' death is not the end of His story?

_____

_____

Why do believers not need proof of Jesus' resurrection, even though the proof exists?

_____

_____

What are you looking forward to about being in heaven?

_____

_____

Keep This in Mind

And also that He might deliver and completely set free all those who through the [haunting] fear of death were held in bondage throughout the whole course of their lives.

Hebrews 2:15 AMPC

Dying is something no one can avoid, yet the fear of death afflicts many people. Feeling some fear of the unknown is understandable, but as Hebrews 2:15 says, that fear can hold us in bondage and keep us from enjoying our lives. We know that someday death will come to all of us, but as believers we have assurance of the resurrection and heaven, and that is cause to celebrate!

CLOSING COMMENTS

Setting Your Mind on Victory

It takes courage to grow up and become who you really are.

E. E. Cummings

Now that you have read *Do It Afraid* and worked your way through this study guide, would you agree with E. E. Cummings that "It takes courage to grow up and become who you really are"? On this page or in some other place, take time to write about who you really are and prayerfully think through the courage it will take to become that person. Consider thinking and praying about the person you can become and the things you can do, with God's help, once fear's hold has been broken in your life. I know you can become the person of freedom and strength that God created you to be as the Holy Spirit leads you and helps you. You can live life bravely and enjoy all of it.

Lessons for Your Journey

As you embark on a new and exciting journey of freedom from fear, several principles from *Do It Afraid* will serve you well. You may want to copy this list in your journal or capture a photo of it on your phone so you can refer to these empowering lessons often.

1. God is committed to helping you fulfill His wonderful plan for your life, while the enemy will use fear to keep you from pursuing God's plan and to prevent you from doing things you enjoy.

2. Fear will never completely disappear from your life. The enemy will persist in trying to control you through fear as much as you will allow. Resist fear by not letting it influence you.

3. Once you confront fear, it must back down. Keep confronting it, no matter how long it takes.

4. Regardless of what is happening in your life or in the world around you, God is greater than it is. He loves you, and He is always with you.

5. Freedom from fear does not mean you never *feel* afraid; it means you do not allow fear to control you or influence your decisions. You find freedom by doing what causes you to be afraid—even when you feel fearful.

6. Fear is simply a feeling, and feelings are fickle. You can learn to live beyond your feelings and to live according to the power of God's Word.

7. With God's help, you can confront fear and break its influence over the way you think and live. In Christ, you have the power to choose not to submit to fear or intimidation; you simply need to exercise it.

8. Learning to do certain things while you feel afraid can change the course of your entire life. You'll be amazed at the freedom, strength, and joy that await you on the other side of fear.

9. You can live without fear, because God loves you with a perfect love. You can be confident in His love in every circumstance.

10. Freedom is gained and then maintained by making right choices in little ways day by day. You will conquer fear one small step at a time, and God will give you grace for each step as you take it.

11. In some circumstances, you may feel fear and courage at the same time. When you do, focus on courage instead of fear. Instead of simply praying to overcome your fear, pray that God will fill you with boldness, confidence, and courage. Instead of thinking about what you are afraid of, think about who God is.

12. The only way you can fail at something is to quit trying. As long as you're making an effort to break free from fear, you're moving forward.

Keep This in Mind

Have I not commanded you? Be strong and courageous. Do not be afraid; do not be discouraged, for the Lord your God will be with you wherever you go.

Joshua 1:9

Do you have a real relationship with Jesus?

God loves you! He created you to be a special, unique, one-of-a-kind individual, and He has a specific purpose and plan for your life. And through a personal relationship with your Creator—God—you can discover a way of life that will truly satisfy your soul.

No matter who you are, what you've done, or where you are in your life right now, God's love and grace are greater than your sin—your mistakes. Jesus willingly gave His life so you can receive forgiveness from God and have new life in Him. He's just waiting for you to invite Him to be your Savior and Lord.

If you are ready to commit your life to Jesus and follow Him, all you have to do is ask Him to forgive your sins and give you a fresh start in the life you are meant to live. Begin by praying this prayer...

Lord Jesus, thank You for giving Your life for me and forgiving me of my sins so I can have a personal relationship with You. I am sincerely sorry for the mistakes I've made, and I know I need You to help me live right.

Your Word says in Romans 10:9, "If you declare with your mouth, 'Jesus is Lord,' and believe in your heart that God raised him from the dead, you will be saved" (NIV). I believe You are the Son of God and confess You as my Savior and Lord. Take me just as I am, and work in my heart, making me the person You want me to be. I want to live for You, Jesus, and I am so grateful that You are giving me a fresh start in my new life with You today.

I love You, Jesus!

It's so amazing to know that God loves us so much! He wants to have a deep, intimate relationship with us that grows every day as we spend time with Him in prayer and Bible study. And we want to encourage you in your new life in Christ.

Please visit joycemeyer.org/salvation to request Joyce's book *A New Way of Living*, which is our gift to you. We also have other free resources online to help you make progress in pursuing everything God has for you.

Congratulations on your fresh start in your life in Christ! We hope to hear from you soon.

ABOUT THE AUTHOR

Joyce Meyer is one of the world's leading practical Bible teachers. A *New York Times* bestselling author, Joyce's books have helped millions of people find hope and restoration through Jesus Christ. Joyce's program, *Enjoying Everyday Life*, airs around the world on television, radio, and the Internet. Through Joyce Meyer Ministries, Joyce teaches internationally on a number of topics with a particular focus on how the Word of God applies to our everyday lives. Her candid communication style allows her to share openly and practically about her experiences so others can apply what she has learned to their lives.

Joyce has authored more than 100 books, which have been translated into more than 100 languages, and over 65 million of her books have been distributed worldwide. Bestsellers include *Power Thoughts*; *The Confident Woman*; *Look Great, Feel Great*; *Starting Your Day Right*; *Ending Your Day Right*; *Approval Addiction*; *How to Hear from God*; *Beauty for Ashes*; and *Battlefield of the Mind*.

Joyce's passion to help hurting people is foundational to the vision of Hand of Hope, the missions arm of Joyce Meyer Ministries. Hand of Hope provides worldwide humanitarian outreaches such as feeding programs, medical care, orphanages, disaster response, human trafficking intervention and rehabilitation, and much more—always sharing the love and gospel of Christ.

JOYCE MEYER MINISTRIES
U.S. & FOREIGN OFFICE ADDRESSES

Joyce Meyer Ministries
P.O. Box 655
Fenton, MO 63026
USA
(636) 349-0303

Joyce Meyer Ministries—Canada
P.O. Box 7700
Vancouver, BC V6B 4E2
Canada
(800) 868-1002

Joyce Meyer Ministries—Australia
Locked Bag 77
Mansfield Delivery Centre
Queensland 4122
Australia
(07) 3349 1200

Joyce Meyer Ministries—England
P.O. Box 1549
Windsor SL4 1GT
United Kingdom
01753 831102

Joyce Meyer Ministries—South Africa
P.O. Box 5
Cape Town 8000
South Africa
(27) 21-701-1056

OTHER BOOKS BY JOYCE MEYER

100 Inspirational Quotes
100 Ways to Simplify Your Life
21 Ways to Finding Peace and Happiness
Any Minute
Approval Addiction
The Approval Fix
The Battle Belongs to the Lord
Battlefield of the Mind*
Battlefield of the Mind Bible
Battlefield of the Mind Devotional
Battlefield of the Mind for Kids
Battlefield of the Mind for Teens
Battlefield of the Mind New Testament
Be Anxious for Nothing*
Beauty for Ashes
Being the Person God Made You to Be
Change Your Words, Change Your Life
Colossians: A Biblical Study
The Confident Mom
The Confident Woman
The Confident Woman Devotional
Do It Afraid*
Do Yourself a Favor . . . Forgive
Eat the Cookie . . . Buy the Shoes
Eight Ways to Keep the Devil under Your Feet
Ending Your Day Right
Enjoying Where You Are on the Way to Where You Are Going
Ephesians: A Biblical Study
The Everyday Life Bible
The Everyday Life Psalms and Proverbs
Filled with the Spirit
Galatians: A Biblical Study
Good Health, Good Life
Habits of a Godly Woman
Healing the Soul of a Woman*
Healing the Soul of a Woman Devotional
Hearing from God Each Morning
How to Hear from God*
How to Succeed at Being Yourself
I Dare You
If Not for the Grace of God*

JOYCE MEYER SPANISH TITLES

Belleza en Lugar de Cenizas (Beauty for Ashes)
Buena Salud, Buena Vida (Good Health, Good Life)
Cambia Tus Palabras, Cambia Tu Vida (Change Your Words, Change Your Life)
El Campo de Batalla de la Mente (Battlefield of the Mind)
Como Formar Buenos Habitos y Romper Malos Habitos (Making Good Habits, Breaking Bad Habits)
La Conexión de la Mente (The Mind Connection)
Dios No Está Enojado Contigo (God Is Not Mad at You)
La Dosis de Aprobación (The Approval Fix)
Efesios: Comentario Bíblico (Ephesians: Biblical Commentary)
Empezando Tu Día Bien (Starting Your Day Right)
Hágalo con Miedo (Do It Afraid)
Hazte un Favor a Ti Mismo…Perdona (Do Yourself a Favor…Forgive)
Madre Segura de Sí Misma (The Confident Mom)
Pensamientos de Poder (Power Thoughts)
Sanidad para el Alma de una Mujer (Healing the Soul of a Woman)
Santiago: Comentario Bíblico (James: Biblical Commentary)
Sobrecarga (Overload)*
Sus Batallas Son del Señor (Your Battles Belong to the Lord)
Termina Bien tu Día (Ending Your Day Right)
Usted Puede Comenzar de Nuevo (You Can Begin Again)
Viva Valientemente (Living Courageously)

BOOKS BY DAVE MEYER

Life Lines

*Study Guide available for this title